True to Your Roots

Carla Kelly

True to Your Roots

Vegan Recipes to Comfort and Nourish You

Arsenal Pulp Press ✦ Vancouver

ARSENAL PULP PRESS
Suite 202–211 East Georgia St.
Vancouver, BC V6A 1Z6
Canada
arsenalpulp.com

The publisher gratefully acknowledges the support of the Government of Canada (through the Canada Book Fund) and the Government of British Columbia (through the Book Publishing Tax Credit Program) for its publishing activities.

Canadä

The author and publisher assert that the information contained in this book is true and complete to the best of their knowledge. All recommendations are made without the guarantee on the part of the author and publisher. The author and publisher disclaim any liability in connection with the use of this information. For more information, contact the publisher.

Note for our UK readers: measurements for non-liquids are for volume, not weight.

Design and cover illustration by Gerilee McBride
All photographs, prop syling, and food styling by Tracey Kusiewicz / Foodie Photography
Editing by Robyn So and Susan Safyan

Printed and bound in Canada

Library and Archives Canada Cataloguing in Publication

Kelly, Carla, 1971–, author
True to your roots : vegan recipes to comfort and nourish
you / Carla Kelly.

Includes index.
Issued in print and electronic formats.
ISBN 978-1-55152-588-4 (paperback).—ISBN 978-1-55152-589-1 (epub)

1. Vegan cooking. 2. Cookbooks. I. Title.

TX837.K455 2015   641.5'636   C2015-903458-2
                                             C2015-903459-0

Dedication

For my daughters, who truly are growing into the young adults
I have always hoped they would.

"You always make the BEST potatoes": my daughter M, age 13.

"This is better than ketchup!" (about the Rutabaga Pizza/Pasta Sauce,
p. 186),: my daughter R, age 10.

Contents

Preface

I am pleased to send this, my fourth book-baby, out into the world for your reading and dining pleasure. In *True to Your Roots*, I celebrate the humble root vegetable in all its many and varied incarnations. I hope readers will learn a little about these underappreciated plants and be introduced to some new favorites. My wish is that these dishes will expand the repertoire of home cooks and also introduce them to new and appealing vegetables. Root vegetables really are much more than mash.

Every recipe in this book has been tested by my team of international recipe testers (and by many of my friends and neighbors), so each recipe will be both tasty and foolproof. The recipes have been approved by vegans and non-vegans alike. However, remaining true to my personally held beliefs and ethics, the recipes are all vegan as well as healthy (health-focused but not -obsessed) and packed with flavor.

For too long the last chosen and least loved, the "ugly vegetables" are now rising up and claiming their rightful place at the center of the plate. In the recipes that follow, I showcase these nutritional and flavorful powerhouses in a variety of tasty and satisfying ways: healthy breakfast juices, sinfully rich desserts, traditional hot side dishes, refreshing and innovative salads, hearty soups, and some eye-popping, mouth-watering main courses. This book truly has something to tempt everyone to go back to their roots.

—Carla

Introduction

While the focus in this book is on vegetables—be they taproots, tubers, rhizomes, corms, or stems—that grow underground, I also include some that grow underwater or aboveground. At the same time, I haven't included roots such as salsify, parsley root, and wasabi because they are harder to find in North America.

I employ a "root to tip" style of cooking (where possible), staying true to the flavors and form of the whole plant and using the greens and leaves of the vegetables in many recipes as well. I am frequently influenced by the ingredients; often, after making a recipe and tasting the ingredients in one context, I find inspiration and ideas for using them in other contexts.

Basic Botany

Root vegetables are the swollen parts of biennial (a two-year biological life cycle) and perennial (longer than two-year life span) plants that act as storage facilities for sugars and starches to provide the energy required for either germination or reproduction. As such, roots are packed with macronutrients required for growth (mainly carbohydrates with protein) and micronutrients (vitamins and minerals) to aid in the plants' development. These macro- and micronutrients are valuable to us as sources of fuel and for our own health and wellbeing.

True root vegetables are those where nutrient storage occurs in the taproot (a single substantial root) of the plant. These come in three shapes:

- conical (wide at top, tapering like a cone): e.g., carrot and parsnip
- fusiform (widest in the middle): e.g., radish and rutabaga
- napiform (wide at top, tapering suddenly): e.g., turnip and beets

I have also included:

- tubers (underground swollen stems or roots): e.g., potatoes and sweet potatoes

- rhizomes (underground / underwater stems growing horizontally): e.g., lotus root

- corms (short vertical underground stem with scale-like leaves): e.g., water chestnut and taro

- stems (aboveground): e.g., kohlrabi

Many of the root vegetables are related botanically, albeit distantly, and share a common origin.

Choosing and Storing Root Vegetables

Whether you're buying them from a supermarket, health-food store, specialty ethnic market, fruit and vegetable store, or farmer's market, or having them delivered to your home, you want to ensure that the vegetables you purchase are giving you the best bang for your buck.

Fresh roots should feel firm and pleasantly solid in your hand. The skin should be taut. Avoid bruised roots with spongy or soft spots. Reject roots with slime, brown patches, cracks, sprouting eyes, or shoots. Extra-large roots may be woody inside (especially parsnips, celeriac, and carrots), so stick to those that are small to medium-large, even if you need to purchase more than one. Smell the root; the aroma should be earthy, not sour or musty.

Organic roots, those grown without pesticides or artificial chemicals, are a wonderful option. Organics are guaranteed not to be genetically modified as well. However, they are pricier and not always available.

Roots stay fresher longer when stored in a cool, dark, dry, and well-ventilated space. If, like me, you don't have a root cellar in your home, the next best place is the basement (or garage) which, while cool, is

The following root vegetables—by far the majority of those available—are suitable for eating raw, juicing, and dehydrating: carrots, beets, sweet potatoes (white- and orange-fleshed), jicama, celeriac, turnips, rutabagas, parsnips, radishes, daikon, sunchokes, kohlrabi, water chestnuts, oca, burdock, horseradish.

Never eat the following roots unless they are completely cooked to destroy the toxins: potatoes, yuca, tropical yams, taro, lotus root.

never cold enough to freeze. It's best to keep roots protected from heat-producing appliances (e.g., the refrigerator or stove) and covered with cloth (or inside a cloth bag) to keep them away from excess light. Although roots can be stored in the crisper drawer of the refrigerator, they usually last longer and retain their flavor stored in a cool, dry place. As a general rule of thumb, if your grocery store does not refrigerate the vegetables, you shouldn't either (unless they have been cut). The majority of roots are best used within a week after purchase.

If buying your roots with greens attached (please do—just make sure the greens are edible, p. 195), remove greens before storing, as they will draw moisture from the root. They also tend to spoil faster. Wrap the greens in paper and store in the crisper; use within two to three days.

Growing Your Own

There are few things more satisfying than creating dinner from ingredients you pulled from the ground in your own backyard. If you have a vegetable patch at home, in a shared plot, or in a community garden, you may already grow some form of root vegetable. While some take longer to mature—rutabagas and parsnips for example—and some are a little trickier to grow—such as celeriac and potatoes—roots are, on the whole, relatively fast-growing and provide a lot of produce with little effort.

Even if you don't have a grassed yard to turn into a vegetable patch, or you have limited experience with gardening, you can easily grow some varieties of roots in deep containers or pots on a patio or balcony—any space which gets sun for most of the day. Choose roots you like to eat, buy some seeds (heirloom varieties have interesting colors and shapes), read the planting and care instructions, and off you go.

Good roots for beginner gardens are radishes, carrots, and beets, as they grow quickly and have widespread appeal. And because you can eat both the roots and leaves raw and cooked, nothing goes to waste.

Waste Not—Root to Tip Usage

Don't throw out the greens attached to your roots. Many are edible—and tasty to boot. A number of the recipes that follow make use of commonly found greens, from those of beets and carrots to kohlrabi. See p. 195 for a list of nontoxic, edible greens.

If the produce is organic and the recipe specifies peeling (for presentation reasons, mainly), it's entirely up to you whether or not to peel, as long as the skin is edible. If produce is not organic, and you prefer to leave the peel on, always wash and scrub the roots to remove any traces of soil. When peeling the roots, also peel the visible "inner skin" or second layer of pigment, if there is one. You'll end up with less flesh, but this second layer is often as inedible as the skin.

Compost all the peels you don't want to use. This keeps biodegradable matter out of the garbage and allows nutrients in the peels and trimmings to be returned to the soil. Check if your municipality has a "green waste" collection program, or use community compost bins. You can also create compost for use in your own garden; starter bins (with detailed instructions) are easily purchased wherever gardening supplies are sold.

↪ If you choose to peel skin that's edible, use the peels to make stock.

Keep a container or large resealable bag in your freezer to which you can add root vegetable peels, onion skins, and trimmings from greens. The only provisos I'd make are to limit the use of trimmings from the Brassica family, as they make the stock distinctly cabbage-y and, unless you want a pink stock, avoid beets.

When you have about 6 cups (1.5 L), place peels and trimmings in a large soup pot, cover with water, bring to a simmer on medium-low heat, and cook for up to an hour, until very tender and almost falling apart. Strain the stock, pressing the trimmings against the strainer to extract all the liquid. Taste and season your stock as desired.

If not using immediately, freeze in 1 cup (250 mL) measures for use in recipes.

About the Ingredients

The availability of ingredients will depend on your location and the season. I make suggestions for substitutions in recipes where relevant, and a list can also be found under the heading, "What to Use Instead" (p. 15).

I've focused on roots that will be easy to find in local supermarkets, fruit and vegetable stores, large grocery chains, health-food stores, and Asian grocers. I like to know that the ingredients can be found close to home, even while I like to expand my comfort zone by experimenting with new ingredients.

- flours; e.g., potato, chickpea, other gluten-free flours
- durum wheat semolina for making pasta and gnocchi
- potato starch (see textbox, p. 23)
- umami sources; e.g., nutritional yeast, liquid smoke, Marmite

→ *What to Use Instead? Some Truly Sensible Substitutions*

If you're stumped about sourcing one of the lesser known roots in a recipe, and neither the description in the appendix nor a Google search has helped, then make one of the substitutions listed below and enjoy the recipe anyway.

- burdock: sunchoke or parsnip
- daikon: radish (plain or other variety)
- lotus root: water chestnut or jicama
- oca: sunchoke, fingerling potato, canned olluco
- sunchoke: fingerling (or other waxy) potato
- taro: white-fleshed sweet potato
- tropical yam: yuca or white-fleshed sweet potato
- water chestnut: canned water chestnut or jicama
- yuca: white-fleshed sweet potato

- alcohol; e.g., sauvignon blanc, merlot, lager (substitute an equal amount of stock or broth in savory recipes and apple juice or non-dairy milk in dessert recipes)
- Asian noodles; e.g., rice sticks (medium size), soba (buckwheat), udon (or long thin pasta, if you prefer)
- vinegar; e.g., balsamic, white balsamic, apple cider
- sweeteners; e.g., agave syrup, brown rice syrup
- nuts and seeds; e.g., nut butters, tahini (feel free to substitute for preferences or allergies)
- spices and seasonings; e.g., smoked paprika, sumac, ground fennel seed
- grains; e.g., red quinoa, sushi rice, steel cut oats, regular and Israeli couscous
- commercial dairy replacements; e.g., almond, rice, or soy milks (purchased or homemade)

Where I call for neutral-flavored oil, I mean all-purpose cooking oil, such as canola, sunflower, safflower, or grapeseed. Other oils are specified as needed. Should you wish to sauté without oil, use a water sauté method instead.

Some aromatics that are often considered root vegetables including *Alliums* (bulbs), such as onions, garlic, and shallots, as well as ginger (a rhizome), find a place in many of the recipes in this book.

When roots are to be grated, I use a coarse grate (on the larger holes on a box grater). Recipes will specify when a fine grate is called for.

Equipment

The following items are useful for making the recipes in this book.

Must-have:

- very sharp knife

- potato masher
- potato peeler
- box grater
- food processor
- blender

Nice-to-have:

- immersion blender for blending soup or stock in the pot
- mandoline for creating perfectly thin, consistently even slices (though a sharp knife and steady hand will do the job)
- juicer for extracting the juice from hard vegetables
- slow cooker (To make slow cooker recipes on the stovetop or in the oven, a general rule of thumb is to use a quarter of the time and double the liquid; however, the recipes in this book haven't been tested with this cooking method, so results may vary.)

Allergens & Icons

cn   contains peanuts, tree nuts, or nut products

gf   gluten-free ingredients

raw   uncooked or individual ingredients heated to less than 115°F (46°C)

Always read labels for potential allergens, as the notation in a recipe does not guarantee an allergen-free dish.

↳ *What's In a Name?*

Where you're from will influence what you call a "sweet potato" and a "yam." For the purposes of this book, and to stop me from going crazy, I'm relying on botany to provide me with the answers.

What is known as a yam in the US and Canada is, botanically, *Ipomoea batatas*, an orange-fleshed version of a sweet potato. I call them sweet potatoes. Because sweet potatoes are readily available with white or orange flesh, I specify white-fleshed or orange-fleshed sweet potatoes in the recipes.

A true yam, genus *Dioscorea*, is a tropical root vegetable and is much longer, denser, and starchier than a sweet potato. There are many varieties of yams throughout Africa, Asia, and the Caribbean; the variety available to you will depend on what your store brings in. For the recipes in this book, use any true yam where I ask for tropical yam.

Truly Nourishing Breakfasts, Brunches & Baking

The first meal of the day may not be what springs to mind when you think of root vegetables—but don't rule it out. For a nutrition-packed beginning to the morning, there are delicious baked goods, and for that lazy Sunday, tempting hot items, including pancakes and waffles.

Carrot Raisin Bran Muffins

Two of the most beloved muffin flavors combined into one perfect breakfast treat. The sweet bursts from the raisins are a delight.

Preheat oven to 375°F (190°C). Line a 12-cup muffin tin with paper liners, or apply non-stick spray.

In a medium bowl, place raisins and grated carrot, and add boiling water to cover by 1 in (2.5 cm). Let soak for 15 minutes. Drain, reserving ½ cup (125 mL) raisin water and setting aside raisins and carrots.

In a large bowl, whisk together flour, bran, baking powder, baking soda, salt, cinnamon, and allspice.

In a small bowl, whisk milk, applesauce, brown sugar, maple syrup, and vanilla extract. Add reserved raisin water. Stir in soaked raisins and carrots.

Add wet ingredients to dry ingredients and mix to just combine. Spoon batter into prepared muffin tin. The cups will be full. Bake for 20–25 minutes, until a toothpick inserted in center of a muffin comes out clean. Cool in tin for 5 minutes, then transfer to a rack to cool completely.

Makes 12 muffins

1/2 cup (125 mL) dark raisins

1/4 cup (60 mL) golden raisins

1 packed cup (250 mL) peeled and finely grated carrots

2 1/4 cups (530 mL) whole wheat pastry flour

1/2 cup (125 mL) wheat bran

3 tsp baking powder

1 tsp baking soda

1/2 tsp salt

1/2 tsp cinnamon

1/4 tsp allspice

1 cup (250 mL) nondairy milk

1/4 cup (60 mL) unsweetened applesauce

1/2 cup (125 mL) brown sugar

2 tbsp maple syrup

1 tsp vanilla extract

Sweet Potato, Pecan & Quinoa Muffins

Hearty and satisfying. Makes you want to find an open fire to sit around while you eat these —after spending the morning trudging through autumn leaves with your dog.

Makes 12 muffins

1 cup (250 mL) nondairy milk
1 1/4 tsp apple cider vinegar

1 1/2 cups (375 mL) spelt or whole wheat
  pastry flour
3/4 cup (175 mL) quinoa flour
3/4 cup (175 mL) ground pecans
2 1/2 tsp baking powder
1 tsp cinnamon
1/2 tsp baking soda
1/2 tsp salt

1 1/4 cups (310 mL) baked and mashed
  orange-fleshed sweet potatoes
3/4 packed cup (175 mL) light brown sugar
1/2 cup (125 mL) cooked quinoa, cooled
3 tbsp neutral-flavored oil
1 tsp vanilla extract

3/4 cup (175 mL) pecan pieces (toasting
  optional)

1/4 cup (60 mL) pecan pieces for garnish
  (optional)

Preheat oven to 375°F (190°C). Line a 12-cup muffin tin with paper liners, or apply non-stick spray.

In a large bowl, combine milk and cider vinegar. Let sit 5 minutes to curdle.

In a medium bowl, sift together flours, ground pecans, baking powder, cinnamon, baking soda, and salt.

To soured milk in bowl, add mashed sweet potatoes, brown sugar, cooked quinoa, oil, and vanilla extract. Mix gently until smooth.

Add dry ingredients to wet ingredients and mix to just combine. Fold in ¾ cup (175 mL) pecan pieces. Spoon batter into prepared muffin tin. The cups will be full. Garnish each with 1 tsp pecan pieces, if desired.

Bake for 30–35 minutes, until a toothpick inserted in center of a muffin comes out clean. Cool in tin for 5 minutes, then transfer to a rack to cool completely.

Canned sweet potatoes may be used in place of cooked, mashed sweet potatoes.

Potato Biscuits gf

Inspired by southern biscuits, Scottish tattie scones, and Irish potato farls bread, these are lovely as stand-alone breakfasts or snacks, or served with stews, soups, or casseroles. You don't need the luck o' the Irish with this simple recipe—just plan ahead and save some mashed potatoes.

Preheat oven to 375°F (190°C). Line a baking sheet with parchment paper.

In a small bowl, combine milk and cider vinegar. Let sit 5 minutes to curdle.

Wrap grated potatoes in a clean tea towel. Squeeze the towel as you roll it around the inside of your sink to remove as much moisture as possible. You should end up with about ¾ cup (175 mL) potatoes. Place in a large bowl. Add mashed potatoes, coconut oil, chives, and soured milk. Mix well.

Sift oat, rice, and potato flours, potato starch, baking powder, salt, baking soda, and black pepper into potato mixture. Mix to combine. Knead gently, until dough holds together.

Turn out onto a lightly floured board. Shape into an 8 x 14-in (20 x 35-cm) rectangle. Cut into 12 2-in (5-cm) squares and transfer to prepared baking sheet. Lightly brush tops with nondairy milk.

Bake for 25–28 minutes, until bottoms are golden, tops are lightly browned, and biscuits look puffy and tender. Cool for 5 minutes on sheet, then transfer to rack to cool completely.

Make your own oat flour by grinding an equal amount of quick-cooking rolled oats in a spice grinder until it forms a powder.

Makes 12 biscuits

1 cup (250 mL) unsweetened nondairy milk
1 1/2 tsp apple cider vinegar

1 cup (250 mL) packed grated white or
  Yukon Gold potatoes (peeling optional)

1 cup (250 mL) mashed potatoes
1/4 cup (60 mL) melted coconut oil
3 tbsp finely chopped chives

1 cup (250 mL) oat flour (see p. 28)
1/2 cup (125 mL) rice flour
1/2 cup (125 mL) potato flour
2 tbsp potato starch
2 tsp baking powder
1 tsp salt
1/2 tsp baking soda
1/4 tsp freshly ground black pepper

1 tbsp nondairy milk

↱ *Potato Starch and Potato Flour*

Both potato flour and starch are usually found in the natural or organics aisle in major supermarkets but are not inter-changeable—so what's the difference?

Potato flour is made from cooked potatoes that are dried and ground, so the flour contains fiber and protein, as well as carbohydrate. It has an off-white, slightly yellow or gray hue and adds a subtle potato flavor. This gluten-free flour is best used in conjunction with other flours.

Potato starch is made from pulped raw potatoes that are repeatedly washed to remove the fiber and protein, leaving pure carbohydrate. It's a white, chalky powder that works as a thickening agent, similar to cornstarch. To prevent clump-ing when it's added to a liquid, make a slurry by dissolving potato starch in a little water. Add to liquid by pouring in a slow stream while stirring or whisking the hot liquid. If you can't find potato starch, use an equal amount of arrowroot powder or cornstarch for similar results.

Turnip, Ginger & Pecan Toffee Scones

Make these a quick-to-put-together breakfast treat by preparing the turnip nut toffee in advance and keeping it in the refrigerator until needed. Feel free to use another nut or nut mixture you prefer.

Make the toffee

Line a large plate with parchment paper.

In a large frying pan on medium-high heat, toast turnips, pecans, and ginger, stirring frequently until turnips are dry-looking and mixture is browned, about 7 minutes. Take care not to burn, especially in the last few minutes.

Add brown sugar and brown rice syrup, stirring constantly to coat turnips and pecans as sugar melts, about 2 minutes. Stir carefully, taking great care with boiling sugar.

Remove from heat and transfer to parchment-lined plate. Refrigerate for 1 hour to cool and firm up. The toffee will remain soft and sticky.

Make the scones

Preheat oven to 375°F (190°C). Line a large baking sheet with parchment paper.

In a large bowl, sift together flours, brown sugar, baking powder, baking soda, salt, ginger, and cinnamon.

Tear toffee into small pieces. Add to dry ingredients and toss to coat. Make a well. Add milk, oil, and vanilla and stir to just combine. Using a ⅓ cup (80 mL) measuring cup prepared with non-stick spray, scoop dough onto prepared tray.

Bake for 18–22 minutes, until firm and bottoms are golden and lightly browned. Cool for 5 minutes on sheet, then transfer to rack to cool completely.

Makes 10 scones

2 cups (500 mL) peeled and grated turnips
1 cup (250 mL) roughly chopped pecans
1-in (2.5-cm) length fresh ginger, peeled and finely grated

3/4 cup (175 mL) brown sugar
1/4 cup (60 mL) brown rice syrup

2 cups (500 mL) whole wheat pastry flour
1 cup (250 mL) all-purpose flour
1/4 cup (60 mL) brown sugar
3 tsp baking powder
1/2 tsp baking soda
1/2 tsp salt
1/2 tsp ground ginger
1/4 tsp ground cinnamon

1 1/4 cups (310 mL) nondairy milk
1/4 cup (60 mL) neutral-flavored oil
1/2 tsp vanilla extract

Carrot Cake Pancakes gf

Bursting with familiar spices, this rustic, old-fashioned pancake is not overly sweet. Serve with maple syrup.

Makes 8 6-in (15-cm) pancakes

Note: Juicer needed

1/2 cup (125 mL) grated carrots
1 cup (250 mL) quick-cooking rolled oats
1/4 cup (60 mL) currants
1/4 cup (60 mL) walnuts, finely chopped

1/2 cup (125 mL) carrot juice, from 2
  medium carrots (or commercially
  prepared)
12 oz (340 g) firm silken or soft tofu
1/2 cup (125 mL) + 1 tbsp unsweetened
  nondairy milk
2/3 cup (160 mL) chickpea flour
1/4 cup (60 mL) confectioner's sugar
2 tbsp potato starch
1 tsp baking powder
1 tsp ground cinnamon
1/2 tsp ground coriander
1/2 tsp salt
1/2 tsp ground nutmeg
1/4 tsp ground cardamom
1/8 tsp ground cloves
1/8 tsp ground allspice

3 tbsp coconut oil, or as required

In a large bowl, combine carrots, rolled oats, currants, and walnuts.

In a blender, combine carrot juice, tofu, milk, chickpea flour, confectioner's sugar, potato starch, baking powder, cinnamon, coriander, salt, nutmeg, cardamom, cloves, and allspice. Blend until thick, smooth, and creamy, stopping to scrape down sides of bowl as required. Pour into grated carrot mix and stir to combine. Let sit 5 minutes.

In a large non-stick frying pan on medium, heat ½ tbsp oil. Scoop scant ½ cup (125 mL) batter into pan and spread to form a thin 6-in (15-cm) round pancake. Cook for 2 minutes, until bubbles appear, the pancake looks dry around edges, and underside is golden brown. Flip carefully and cook for 2 more minutes. Repeat until all batter is used.

Sweet Potato Pie Waffles

I call these "Pie Waffles" because the uncooked batter tastes just like sweet potato pie filling.

In a large bowl, combine milk and cider vinegar. Let sit 5 minutes to curdle. Add sweet potatoes, brown sugar, oil, and vanilla extract. Whisk to combine.

Sift flours, baking powder, and pie spice into sweet potato mixture. Whisk to combine. Let batter rest while waffle maker heats.

Spray inside plates of waffle maker with non-stick spray before making each waffle and cook according to manufacturer's instructions.

Makes 6 8-in (20-cm) waffles

1 cup (250 mL) + 2 tbsp nondairy milk
2 tsp apple cider vinegar

3/4 cup (175 mL) baked, mashed orange-
   fleshed sweet potatoes (or canned)
3/4 packed cup (175 mL) light brown sugar
1/2 cup (125 mL) neutral-flavored oil
1 tsp vanilla extract

1 1/4 cups (310 mL) all-purpose flour
1/2 cup (125 mL) whole wheat pastry flour
2 tsp baking powder
1 tsp pumpkin pie spice

Bircher Muesli Parsnip Breakfast Loaf

This is loosely based on the traditional Swiss breakfast, which is made with loads of cream and yogurt, as well as oats, raisins, and apples. The loaf has flavor and just enough sweetness to be a healthy breakfast treat. If you like things a little sweeter, add 2 tbsp granulated sugar with the agave syrup.

Makes 1 9-in (23-cm) loaf

3/4 cup (175 mL) cored and grated Granny Smith apples (peeling optional)

1/2 cup (125 mL) peeled and grated parsnip

3/4 cup (175 mL) nondairy creamer

1/2 cup (125 mL) agave syrup

1/2 cup (125 mL) quick-cooking rolled oats (not instant)

1/2 cup (125 mL) plain nondairy yogurt

2 tbsp lemon juice

2 tbsp apple juice

1/2 cup (125 mL) all-purpose flour

1/2 cup (125 mL) whole wheat pastry flour

1/2 cup (125 mL) oat flour

3 tsp baking powder

3/4 tsp baking soda

3/4 tsp ground cinnamon

1/2 teaspoon salt

1/4 tsp ground nutmeg

1/2 cup (125 mL) quick-cooking rolled oats

2/3 cup (160 mL) raisins or chopped dried fruit of choice

In a large bowl, combine apples, parsnips, creamer, agave syrup, rolled oats, yogurt, and lemon and apple juices. Mix, cover, and place in refrigerator for a minimum of 2 hours, preferably overnight.

Preheat oven to 350°F (180°C). Line a 9 x 5-in (2 L) loaf pan with parchment paper.

Remove soaked oat mixture from refrigerator and let sit 15 minutes to come to room temperature, as the oven heats.

To oat mixture, sift in flours, baking powder, baking soda, cinnamon, salt, and nutmeg. Mix to combine well. Stir in dry quick-cooking oats and raisins. Spoon batter into prepared loaf pan. It will be about three-quarters full.

Bake for 45–50 minutes, until golden brown with darker edges and a toothpick inserted in center of loaf comes out clean. Some pieces of fruit may cling to toothpick. Cool for 10 minutes in pan, then transfer to rack to cool completely.

If you can't find oat flour in the store, make your own. Put quick-cooking rolled oats in a food processor and pulse to a flour-like consistency (one measure oats will make one measure oat flour). This may not sift as easily as commercial flour; just stir in the unsifted bits.

To make preparation really easy, soak oat mix overnight and bake in the morning, or set to soak all day and bake loaf in the evening.

The soaked oat mixture also makes a tasty breakfast as is.

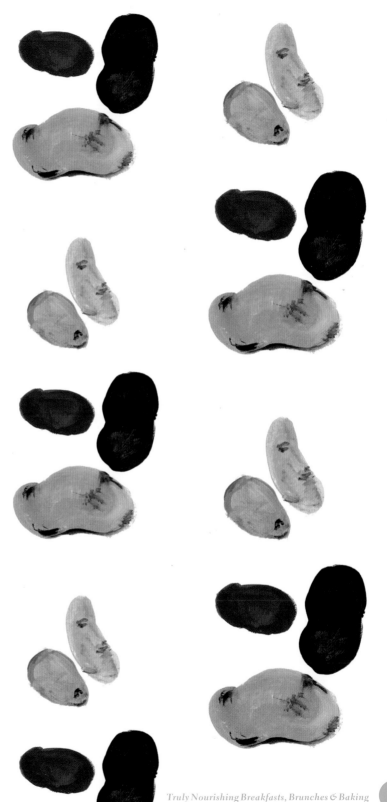

➡ *When Is a Potato Not a Potato? Or, All Potatoes Are Not Created Equal*

Just when you thought things were simple, it turns out there are differences between potatoes.

- Waxy potatoes, such as fingerlings, have thin skin and firm flesh that hold their shape when cooked. They don't easily fall apart and remain creamy and smooth. Best used for salads, grilling, and roasting.

- Starchy potatoes, such as russets (a.k.a. Idaho potatoes), have a high starch content and airy flesh that can absorb a lot of liquid and remain fluffy. Best used for baking, mashing, and French fries.

- Yukon Gold, white, and red potatoes are the go-to spuds for most people and most recipes. Best used for pretty much anything you can use a potato for.

- Purple or blue potatoes can be waxy or starchy, depending on the variety, and in most instances can be used in place of white and red potatoes for an interesting splash of color.

- New potatoes (a.k.a. baby potatoes) are harvested before fully mature. At this stage, their flesh is firm and creamy.

- Potatoes with green patches have been exposed to light and developed a toxin called solanine, which is harmful. Green potatoes may be poisonous and should not be eaten.

Fermented Potato Bread

Fragrant and soft, with a chewy crust and pronounced tang, this Māori bread is wonderful hot from the oven and slathered with margarine, or sliced for sandwiches or toast. Traditionally made in a deep-sided pot, you can also use an 8-in (2-L) oven-safe pot. Start the recipe the day before, as the potato starter needs to ferment for 24 hours.

Makes 1 8-in (2-L) round loaf

1/2 cup (125 mL) hot tap water (110–115°F)
1 tsp sugar

1 medium white or Yukon Gold potato,
  peeled and grated
1 tsp active dry yeast

1/2 cup (125 mL) mashed potatoes, warm or
  room temperature
1 tsp salt

1 1/2 cups (375 mL) all-purpose flour
1 1/2 tbsp potato starch

1 cup (250 mL) all-purpose flour, divided

Ferment potatoes

In a large bowl, combine warm water and sugar and stir to dissolve. Add grated potatoes, and stir in yeast. Cover with a clean tea towel. Let sit for 24 hours at room temperature. Yeast mixture will look frothy and potatoes will soften. If you can't proceed with recipe after 24 hours, place in refrigerator. Return to room temperature before continuing. May be stored in refrigerator for up to 48 hours.

Make bread dough

To fermented potatoes, add mashed potatoes and salt. Stir to combine.

Stir in flour and potato starch. Knead lightly in bowl to combine. Cover bowl and let sit in a warm place for 30 minutes. Stir in an additional ½ cup (125 mL) all-purpose flour. Knead in bowl to combine, cover again, and let sit in warm place for 30 minutes.

Lightly grease an 8-in (20-cm) springform pan.

Turn dough onto lightly floured board and knead in remaining ½ cup (125 mL) flour. Continue to knead for 10 minutes, until dough is smooth and elastic. Shape into 8-in (20-cm) disc and place into prepared pan. Return to warm place to rise for 45 minutes. During last 15 minutes of rising, preheat oven to 400°F (200°C).

Score top of dough with an "X." Bake for 35–40 minutes, until golden and bread sounds hollow when removed from pan and tapped. Cool for 5 minutes in pan. Transfer to rack to cool completely.

Mixed Fruited Root Vegetables

Sweet roasted root vegetables are made just a little bit sweeter with the addition of chopped dried fruits. You may think it sounds strange, but don't knock it 'til you try it.

Makes 4–6 servings

1 medium white- or orange-fleshed sweet potato, peeled and cut into 1-in (2.5-cm) cubes

4 medium white or Yukon Gold potatoes, cut into 1-in (2.5-cm) cubes (peeling optional)

1/2 medium rutabaga, peeled and cut into 1-in (2.5-cm) cubes

2 or 3 medium parsnips, peeled and cut into 1/2-in (1-cm) cubes

1 medium onion, root end left on, peeled and cut into 6 equal wedges

6 garlic cloves, peeled

1 1/2 tbsp olive oil

pinch each salt and pepper

1/2 cup (125 mL) dried apple slices, roughly chopped

1/4 cup (60 mL) dried plums, roughly chopped

1/4 cup (60 mL) dried apricots, roughly chopped

1 tbsp olive oil

Preheat oven to 400°F (200°C). Line a large baking sheet with parchment paper.

Toss vegetables in 1 ½ tbsp olive oil to coat. Spread in a single layer on a baking sheet, and sprinkle with salt and pepper to taste.

Roast for 30 minutes, until tender and beginning to brown. Add dried fruits and 1 tbsp olive oil to roasted vegetables, toss to combine, and roast for 15 minutes, until fruits have softened and vegetables are very tender and golden.

There are 6 wedges of onion and 6 cloves of garlic so ideally each person will get at least 1 of each.

The parsnips are cut a little smaller than the other vegetables, as they're denser and take longer to cook until tender.

Leaving the root end on the onion holds the layers together as they cook, making serving easier.

Substitute dried fruits with raisins or dried cranberries, if you prefer.

Carrots make a good substitute for any of the root vegetables.

Potato, Daikon & Sweet Potato Strata

The perfect way to introduce the mellow delights of cooked daikon. This strata is warm, comforting, and familiar, even with the addition of this less well-known vegetable.

Preheat oven to 375°F (190°C). Lightly oil an 11 x 7-in (2-L) glass baking dish.

In a medium frying pan on medium, heat oil and margarine until bubbly. Add white and light green parts of spring onions and sauté for 2 minutes, until soft. Add potato starch, nutritional yeast, dried mustard, dill, salt, and pepper, and stir for 1 minute. Whisk in milk and stock ½ cup (125 mL) at a time, mixing well after each addition until smooth.

Remove from heat and pour sauce into prepared baking dish. Set aside while preparing the vegetables.

Peel vegetables (optional for potatoes). Using a mandoline, a slicer blade in a food processor, or a very sharp knife, slice vegetables into ⅛-in (3-mm) rounds.

Layer vegetables in sauce in dish in this order: one-third potatoes, all the daikon, one-third potatoes, all the sweet potatoes, remainder of potatoes. Press layers into sauce to partially submerge. Sprinkle top with reserved spring onions.

Cover dish with aluminum foil. Bake for 45 minutes until fork-tender. Increase oven temperature to 425°F (220°C), remove foil, and bake for 15 minutes, until sauce is thick and top is browned.

Switch it up by using any white- or cream-fleshed root vegetable in place of daikon, such as parsnips, sweet potatoes, celeriac, or turnips.

Please take care when using a mandoline to slice vegetables, as it is sharp and can give you a nasty cut.

Makes 4 servings

1 tbsp olive oil
1 tbsp vegan margarine

4 spring onions, finely chopped, darker green parts reserved for garnish

2 tbsp potato starch
1 tbsp nutritional yeast
1 1/4 tsp dried mustard
1 tsp dried dill
1 tsp salt
1/4 tsp freshly ground black pepper

1 1/2 cups (375 mL) unsweetened nondairy milk
1 cup (250 mL) vegetable stock

1 lb (500 g) Yukon Gold potatoes
6 oz (175 g) daikon
1 small white-fleshed sweet potato

Taro Hash Brown Cakes

Simply seasoned, these make a perfect side for any meal from breakfast to dinner. The super starchy nature of taro makes these cakes quite filling.

Makes 8 cakes

1 cup (250 mL) peeled and grated taro

1 cup (250 mL) peeled and grated white or Yukon Gold potatoes

1 shallot, finely grated

1/4 cup (60 mL) potato flour

1/2 tsp salt

1/8 tsp freshly ground black pepper

1/8 tsp red pepper flakes

1/4 cup (60 mL) unsweetened nondairy milk

1 tbsp coconut oil, or more as needed

Bring a medium saucepan of salted water on high heat to a boil. Add grated taro and potatoes, return water to a boil, and cook for 3 minutes to ensure taro is well cooked. This mixture will look like a gloopy mess.

Drain and rinse under cold water until cool, then spread on a clean tea towel to absorb excess water.

In a large bowl, place taro-potato mixture. Add shallots, potato flour, salt, black pepper, and red pepper flakes and mix well. Add milk and mix to just combine. Mixture will be thick and sticky.

In a large frying pan on medium to medium-high, heat oil. With damp hands, form scant ¼-cup (60-mL) measures of mixture into 2-in (5-cm) patties. Place into hot oil, taking care not to overcrowd pan.

Cook for 3 minutes, until golden brown and crisp. Flip and cook second side for 2 more minutes. Repeat until all mixture is used, adding additional oil as needed.

Complete the initial cooking of taro and potatoes in advance for a quick finish.

⤳ True Facts: Taro

Taro is one of a few root vegetables that are toxic when raw. I ensure taro is completely cooked in my recipes, first by cooking it until tender and discarding the cooking water, then by adding the cooked taro to the dish, where it's cooked again.

In the grocery store, you may see two varieties of taro: one is monstrously big with brown flecks in a purplish flesh; the other is small, about the size of a fist, with hairy brown skin. I have used the smaller taro in my recipes, but if you can find only the larger variety use it in the same amount called for in the ingredient list.

Taro has a lovely white flesh that discolors quickly when first cut, so place in water with a little lemon juice if not using immediately. As it cooks, taro changes color to a mild purple hue.

Carrot & Herb Sausages gf

Softer textured than Sunchoke & Mushroom Sausages (p. 38), these gluten-free beauties are bursting with vibrant fresh herb flavors. Serve for breakfast with a hot comfort-food such as Potato, Daikon & Sweet Potato Strata (p. 33), or for lunch or dinner with Turnip & Cauliflower Mash (p. 136) or Kalecannon & Avocado (p. 129).

Makes 8 sausages

1 1/4 cups (310 mL) boiling water
1/2 cup (125 mL) TVP granules
2 tbsp ground flaxseeds
2 tbsp tomato paste
1 tsp liquid smoke

1 tbsp olive oil

1 shallot, finely chopped
2 cups (500 mL) peeled and grated carrots

1 tsp ground cumin
1 tsp ground coriander

1/4 cup (60 mL) chickpea flour
1/4 cup (60 mL) potato flour
3 tbsp minced fresh parsley
2 tbsp finely sliced fresh chives
1 tbsp minced cilantro
1 tsp finely chopped fresh thyme
1/2 tsp dried oregano
1/2 tsp dried tarragon
1/2 tsp salt
1/8 tsp freshly ground black pepper

2 tbsp olive oil

In a large bowl, combine boiling water, TVP granules, flaxseeds, tomato paste, and liquid smoke. Stir and cover. Let sit for 20 minutes.

Line a large plate with parchment paper.

In a large frying pan on medium, heat 1 tbsp oil. Sauté shallots and grated carrots for 7 minutes, until soft, lightly browned, and reduced by half in volume. Add cumin and coriander, and sauté 30 seconds more. Transfer to bowl with TVP mixture. Stir in flours, fresh and dried herbs, and salt and pepper to form a moist, thick dough.

With damp hands, shape into eight 4-in (10-cm) long sausages. Place onto prepared plate and chill for at least an hour.

In a large frying pan on medium, heat 2 tbsp oil. Fry sausages for 8–10 minutes, until cooked through, turning to brown all sides.

Sunchoke & Mushroom Sausages

Savory and earthy, this one is for mushroom lovers. It's like having a sausage and sautéed mushrooms at the same time. Lovely when split then grilled, or pan-fried.

Makes 4

1 tbsp olive oil

2 cups (500 mL) coarsely grated cremini
   mushrooms

1 packed cup (250 mL) coarsely grated
   sunchokes, peeling optional

3/4 cup (175 mL) vegetable stock

2 tbsp Marmite

1 tsp yellow mustard

1 tsp dried thyme

1/2 tsp dried oregano

1/4 tsp freshly ground black pepper

2 tbsp chickpea flour

2 tbsp nutritional yeast

3/4 cup (175 mL) + 2 tbsp vital wheat gluten

In a large frying pan on medium, heat oil. Sauté mushrooms and sunchokes for 10 minutes, until soft, starting to brown, and reduced by half in volume.

In a small bowl, mix stock, Marmite, mustard, thyme, oregano, and black pepper. Add to mushrooms in frying pan. Cook for 2 minutes to infuse flavors and dissolve Marmite. Remove from heat and cool to room temperature, about 20 minutes.

Fit medium saucepan with a steamer basket. Add water to reach bottom of basket. Have ready four 6-in (15-cm) long pieces of aluminum foil.

Stir chickpea flour and nutritional yeast in to cooled mushroom mixture. Add vital wheat gluten and mix to combine well. Knead with hands for 3–4 minutes to activate gluten. Divide mixture into 4 equal pieces and shape into logs about 4-in (10-cm) long. Wrap tightly in foil and place in steamer basket.

Cover saucepan, bring water to a boil, then reduce heat to maintain a simmer. Cook for 55–60 minutes, until packages are firm to the touch, adding water to saucepan as needed to keep from boiling dry.

Remove from heat and allow packages to cool until you can unwrap them. If not serving immediately, allow to cool completely before storing in refrigerator.

If bits of grated sunchokes and mushrooms fall out as you shape the sausages — just poke them back in. They will be mostly absorbed by the sausage as it swells and cooks.

→ *True Facts: Sunchokes*

Also known as Jerusalem artichokes (an unfortunate name, as they're neither from the Middle East nor related to the artichoke), they are, in fact, native North American roots of a plant related to the sunflower.

The plant is cultivated for the tubers, which are small and knobbly, with an irregular shape like fresh ginger. Usually light brown in color, they have a crisp texture when raw and a creamy smooth one when cooked.

Truly Simple Juices

Fresh juices capture intense, vibrant flavors that burst onto your palate. You'll need a juicer to get the healthy elixir from those hard roots.

Mix & Match Root Veggie Juices

Any root vegetable which can be eaten raw (see p. 13) is suitable for juicing.
If you want to experiment beyond this collection of juice recipes, here are some pointers.

- Start by juicing softer fruit or vegetables using a slow setting on your juicer, then finish with harder vegetables on a fast setting.

- All root vegetable juices will have an "earthy" quality.

- To make any juice sweeter, add an apple, pear, orange, or carrot, selecting that which will best suit the type of roots in your juice.

- To neutralize excessive spiciness, add an apple, cucumber, celery, or jicama.

- These root vegetable juices are sweet: carrots, beets, and sweet potatoes (both orange- and white-fleshed).

- These root vegetables are neutral: rutabagas, celeriac, parsnips, kohlrabi, and jicama.

- These root vegetables deliver a little a kick to the palate: radish, daikon, and turnips.

- Horseradish is especially potent—use just a little.

Hints for juicing

- There's no need to peel most produce if it's organic, though I recommend peeling nonorganic produce.

- Always peel citrus and other fruits or vegetables with nonedible skins, such as celeriac and mango.

- Core apples and pears, and pit stone fruit and mangoes before juicing.

- Cut produce to fit the feed chute on your juicer.

- Follow manufacturer's instructions for your juicer model.

Makes 2–3 cups (500–750 mL)
—all juices

Note: Juicer needed

Creamy Juice

Creamy in color and creamy in texture. The optional ginger adds zing to this easy drinking juice. Nashi pear is also called Asian pear, Korean pear, apple pear, and brown pear.

2 large Nashi pear, cored
1 small white-fleshed sweet potato
1/2-in (1-cm) length ginger (optional)

Process ingredients through juicer in order listed. Stir to combine. Present with garnish, as desired.

Sweet Potato, Ginger & Apple Juice

Add some zip to your morning! Sweet and rich, but with a definite kick, this juice will help you face your day with pizzazz.

2 large or 3 medium sweet apples, such as Gala, cored
1-in (2.5-cm) length fresh ginger
1 small white-fleshed sweet potato
slice fresh ginger, for garnish

Process ingredients through juicer in order listed. Stir to combine. Present with garnish, as desired.

Carrot, Sweet Potato & Mango Juice

A little out of the ordinary, this is one orange-colored taste explosion.

1 medium mango, seeded and peeled
2 medium carrots
1 small orange-fleshed sweet potato
1 medium sweet apple, such as Gala, cored

Process ingredients through juicer in order listed. Stir to combine. Present with garnish, as desired.

Parsnip, Grapefruit & Orange Juice

The natural tartness of grapefruit is tempered in this smooth, pleasant morning pick-me-up.

1 medium grapefruit, peel and pith removed
2 medium oranges, peeled
1 medium parsnip

Process ingredients through juicer in order listed. Stir to combine. Present with garnish, as desired.

Ruby Red Juice

Bursting with sweetness and not even a hint of earthy beet, this juice will convert even the most sceptical beet-o-phobe.

1 1/2 cups (375 mL) red grapes
1 medium red bell pepper, seeded
1 medium beet

Process ingredients through juicer in order listed. Stir to combine. Present with garnish, as desired.

Turnip, Cucumber & Apple Juice

Crisp and cooling with a hint of sweetness and a surprising burst of spiciness at the end. This juice makes a delightful midday pick-me-up, especially when you feel a little under the weather.

1/2 English cucumber
5 fresh mint leaves
1 large sweet apple, such as Gala, cored
1 medium turnip
1 mint leaf, for garnish

Process ingredients through juicer in order listed. Stir to combine. Present with garnish, as desired.

Pear & Rutabaga Juice

Sometimes Mother Nature knows best—ripening produce that tastes great together at the same time of year.

2 very ripe small pears (or Asian pears), cored
1 Granny Smith apple, cored
1/2 medium turnip
1/4 small rutabaga

Process ingredients through juicer in order listed. Stir to combine. Present with garnish, as desired.

Celeriac & Berry Juice

Pretty blush-pink, with a gentle, sweet flavor.

1/2 cup (125 mL) raspberries
1 cup (250 mL) strawberries, hulled
1 large sweet apple, such as Fuji
1 small celeriac, peeled
1 strawberry, quartered, for garnish

Process ingredients through juicer in order listed. Stir to combine. Present with garnish, as desired.

Jicama & Melon Juice

Sweet and refreshing—wonderful served over ice on a hot day.

1/2 medium cantaloupe melon, peeled and seeded
1 small jicama, peeled

Process ingredients through juicer in order listed. Stir to combine. Present with garnish, as desired.

Daikon, Carrot, Celery & Apple Juice

Sweet and smooth, with a hard-to-place tang at the end, this juice revs you up and nourishes at the same time.

2 medium sweet apples, such as Gala, cored
1 celery stalk, trimmed
2-in (5-cm) length daikon
2 medium carrots

Process ingredients through juicer in order listed. Stir to combine. Present with garnish, as desired.

Spicy Radish, Pepper & Tomato Juice

This reminds me of the spicy vegetable cocktail blend you find on grocery shelves. If you like it sweeter, add a carrot or a second red bell pepper.

3 medium Roma tomatoes
1 celery stalk, trimmed
1 red bell pepper, seeded
1 jalapeño, stem removed (seeding optional)
1 cup (250 mL) scrubbed red radishes, greens removed
2 celery leaves, for garnish

Process ingredients through juicer in order listed. Stir to combine. Present with garnish, as desired.

Kohlrabi, Apple & Pear Juice

Gently refreshing with a sweet tart burst of flavor, this beautiful pale green juice makes a nice midday treat.

2 ripe pears, cored
2 Granny Smith apples, cored
1 large kohlrabi, peeled

Process ingredients through juicer in order listed. Stir to combine. Present with garnish, as desired.

Truly Tasty Starters & Appies

Kick off a meal, have a light lunch, or host a party. These smaller, lighter dishes are great with a buffet or to start a meal. They may introduce you to a new favorite taste sensation.

Roasted Garlic & Celeriac Hummus

Smooth and mild, this dip sings with subtle hints of roasted celeriac. It'll have your guests going back for more, all the while wondering what makes this hummus so good.

Preheat oven to 400°F (200°C).

Pierce skin on celeriac with a fork. Rub cut side with ½ tsp olive oil, and place cut side down on sheet of aluminum foil. Wrap and bake for 40 minutes, until just knife-tender.

Meanwhile, remove papery skin from head of garlic. Slice top off head to expose flesh in bulbs. Place on a piece of foil, drizzle with ½ tsp oil, and wrap. Once celeriac has baked for 40 minutes, add wrapped garlic to oven and bake for 25 minutes, until celeriac is completely tender and garlic is very soft.

Remove celeriac and garlic from oven, unwrap, and let cool for 30 minutes.

Scoop out ¾ cup (175 mL) celeriac flesh and discard skin. Place flesh in food processor bowl.

Squeeze roasted garlic from skins and add to celeriac. Add chickpeas, 3 tbsp water, tahini, salt, cumin, and pepper to food processor. Pulse to combine until smooth, stopping to scrape down sides of bowl as required. Add extra water if needed to reach desired consistency.

Taste and adjust seasoning as desired. Serve chilled or at room temperature.

Makes about 2 ½ cups (125 mL)

1/2 small celeriac, trimmed and cleaned, peel left on
1/2 tsp olive oil

1 head garlic
1/2 tsp olive oil

1 1/2 cups (375 mL) cooked chickpeas, drained and rinsed
2 tbsp tahini
1/2 tsp salt
1/2 tsp ground cumin
1/4 tsp freshly ground black pepper

Roasted Rosemary Slices gf

Perfectly tender on the inside and delightfully crispy on the edges, these thin root veggie slices make an appealing side dish or tasty snack.

Makes 2–4 servings

2 medium carrots, peeled
2 medium parsnips, peeled
4 medium white or Yukon Gold potatoes, peeled

1 1/2 tbsp olive oil
1 tsp salt
1 tsp dried, crumbled rosemary or 1 tbsp finely chopped fresh rosemary
1/2 tsp garlic powder
freshly ground black pepper, to taste

Preheat oven to 400°F (200°C). Line 2 large baking sheets with parchment paper.

Using a mandoline, slicer blade in a food processor, or very sharp knife, slice vegetables on the bias into ⅛-in (3-mm) thick rounds.

Transfer slices to a large bowl, add remaining ingredients, and mix well. Use your hands to coat vegetable slices with oil and spices.

Spread slices in a single layer on baking sheets.

Bake for 15 minutes. Remove from oven and use tongs to flip slices safely and easily. Return trays to oven, switching racks. Bake for 10 more minutes. Repeat flipping and switching process. Bake for 7–8 minutes, until slices are browned and edges are crispy. Adjust cooking time up or down as required.

For best results, slice carrots first and potatoes last to lessen time potatoes are exposed to air.

↪ Chip It, Chip It Good

Follow these tips for making deep-fried root veggie chips. These crispy slivers of tasty root vegetable goodness are loved equally by adults and children and make perfect starters to any meal.

- If you have a deep fryer, then make use of it. If not, heat 2 in (5 cm) neutral-flavored oil to 375°–400°F (190°–200°C) on a deep-fry thermometer in a deep-sided soup pot, and keep it constant. The addition of cold vegetables may lower the temperature, so allow oil to reheat between each batch.

- When prepping veggies for chips, cut evenly so all slices cook for the same amount of time—a mandoline or very sharp knife is helpful for this.

- To avoid hot oil spitting when veggies are added, pat cut vegetables dry using clean kitchen towels.

- Take care when adding vegetable chips to hot oil—use metal (not plastic) tongs or a metal slotted spoon for safety. Add veggie slices to the pot away from you, as they may spit. And carefully place, don't drop, the pieces in.

- Do not overcrowd pot. For best results, fry in small batches. Most chips take 4–5 minutes to become golden brown and crisp and may require turning while frying. Remove chips from hot oil carefully, using metal utensils. Drain on layers of paper towels or brown paper bags to absorb excess oil.

- Season with salt, pepper, and any herbs or spices you fancy while chips are still hot. Toss with care, and also take care when eating—give them a few minutes to cool slightly.

Potato Pizzettes *gf*

Satisfy your pizza craving in a gluten-free way. The crust has crunch at the edges, a soft center, and can be eaten with your hands. Customize the toppings to suit individual preferences.

Makes 6 pizzettes

1 tbsp cornmeal

1 medium Yukon Gold potato (peeling optional)

1/2 tbsp olive oil

3 tbsp Rutabaga Pizza/Pasta Sauce (p. 186) or your favorite

6 tbsp topping of choice, such as sautéed mushrooms, spinach, onions, red bell peppers

1/2 cup (125 mL) grated vegan cheese of choice (optional)

Preheat oven to 450°F (230°C). Line a baking sheet with parchment paper and sprinkle with cornmeal.

Fill a medium saucepan three-quarters with water and bring to a boil. Once water is boiling, use a mandoline, slicer blade in a food processor, or very sharp knife to slice potatoes into ⅛-in (3-mm) rounds. Carefully add rounds to boiling water and return to a boil. Drain.

Using tongs, overlap 5 or 6 rounds onto prepared tray, forming six 4-in (10-cm) circles, like petals of a flower. Try not to overlap the rounds too thickly or they won't crisp evenly. Form 6 pizzettes. Brush tops lightly with oil.

Bake for 10–12 minutes, until edges are dry-looking and starting to curl away from center.

Carefully flip pizzettes. Return to oven and bake 7–8 minutes, until edges are golden and pizzettes look sturdy.

Top each pizzette with ½ tbsp sauce and gently spread to edges. Top with 1 tbsp of your choice of topping and evenly distribute cheese, if using, on pizzettes.

Return to oven and bake 5–7 minutes, until cheese is melted and toppings are heated through. Pizzette bottoms will be crispy and browned.

Rustic Potato & Olive Flatbread

Chewy with a crisp bottom crust, this salty, savory flatbread makes a wonderful starter to a Mediterranean-themed meal. Serve alongside a salad for a simple lunch, or spread with margarine and enjoy warm from the oven.

In a large bowl, combine warm water, syrup, and yeast. Let sit for 10 minutes until bubbly. Stir in grated potatoes, salt, oregano, garlic powder, and lemon juice. Let rest for 10 minutes.

Preheat oven to 425°F (220°C). Line a baking sheet with parchment paper. Sprinkle with 1 tbsp cornmeal. Stir in flours and potato starch. Knead until well mixed, then knead in olives. Let rest for 10 more minutes.

With slightly damp hands, stretch and spread dough onto baking sheet into a ⅛-in (3-mm) thick random shape. Sprinkle with remaining cornmeal.

Bake for 18–20 minutes, until golden underneath, slightly puffed, and firm to the touch.

Use a clean tea towel to squeeze the liquid from the grated potatoes.

Makes 4 servings

1/2 cup (125 mL) warm water
1/2 tbsp brown rice syrup
1 tsp instant yeast

1 medium white or Yukon Gold potato, peeled, finely grated, and all liquid squeezed out
1/2 tsp salt
1/2 tsp dried oregano
1/4 tsp garlic powder
2 tsp lemon juice

2 tbsp cornmeal, divided

3/4 cup (175 mL) gluten-free flour blend
1/2 cup (125 mL) buckwheat flour
2 tbsp potato starch

3 tbsp finely chopped Kalamata olives

2 tbsp cornmeal, divided

Rutabaga Samosas

Typically made with potatoes, samosas pack a flavor punch in a small packet. Enhanced with a range of warming spices, sweet raisins, earthy walnuts, and bright green peas, this rutabaga version will easily become a favorite.

Make filling

In a large frying pan on medium high, melt oil. Sauté rutabagas, onions, jalapeño, and mustard seeds for 5 minutes until onions are golden. Add cumin, coriander, cardamom, salt, turmeric, and pepper. Sauté for 1 minute.

Stir in coconut milk. Add ¼ cup (60 mL) water. Cover and steam for 5 minutes, until rutabaga is just tender and liquid is almost gone. Remove from heat.

Stir in peas, walnuts, raisins, cilantro, and lemon juice. Taste and adjust seasoning as desired. Cool to room temperature while you make dough.

Make dough

Line a plate with paper towels and set aside.

In a small bowl, mix sparkling water and lime juice. Chill in freezer for 5 minutes.

In a large bowl, whisk together flour, salt, turmeric, coriander, and cumin.

Quickly, so the heat of your hands doesn't melt the coconut oil, rub it in to form crumbs. Make a well. Add water and lime juice mixture to well. Mix to combine, then knead gently to form a dough. Cover dough in bowl with a clean towel and let rest 15 minutes.

In a deep fryer or large pot on high, heat 2 in (5 cm) neutral-flavored oil to 375°F (190°C) on a deep-fry thermometer or so that a small piece of dough dropped into hot oil immediately sizzles vigorously. Line a baking sheet with paper towels.

Roll dough ¹⁄₁₆ in (1.5 mm) thick. Cut into 3-in (8-cm) squares. Place 1 tbsp filling in center of each square and fold corner to corner, forming a triangle shape. Pinch all sides to seal and expel air.

Makes 24 samosas

Filling

1 tbsp coconut oil

2 cups (500 mL) diced rutabagas

1 medium onion, finely chopped

1 jalapeño, seeded and finely chopped

1 tsp mustard seeds

1 tsp ground cumin

1 tsp ground coriander

1/2 tsp ground cardamom

1/4 tsp salt

1/8 tsp turmeric

1/8 tsp freshly ground black pepper

3/4 cup (175 mL) coconut milk

1/2 cup (125 mL) frozen peas, thawed

1/4 cup (60 mL) walnut pieces

1/4 cup (60 mL) golden raisins

1/4 cup (60 mL) cilantro leaves, roughly chopped

1 tbsp lemon juice

continued ↳

↳ *Dough*

3/4 cup (175 mL) cold sparkling water
2 tbsp lime juice

3 cups (750 mL) all-purpose flour
1/2 tsp salt
1/4 tsp turmeric
1/8 tsp ground coriander
1/8 tsp ground cumin

1/2 cup (125 mL) firm coconut oil

neutral-flavored oil for cooking

Carefully add samosas, 4 at time, to hot oil, taking care not to overcrowd pot. Cook for 1 ½–2 minutes, turning to cook other side for 1–2 minutes. Using a metal slotted spoon, remove cooked samosas from oil and drain on paper towels.

You can make filling up to 3 days in advance.

If you prefer not to deep-fry, preheat oven to 400°F (200°C) and bake prepared samosas on a lined baking sheet for 20 minutes, turning after 10, until golden.

To ensure your coconut oil is firm, chill at the same time as you chill the liquids.

Onion & Parsnip Bhaji *gf*

Crunchy golden brown outsides with pillowy-soft insides, these Indian street food-themed bites marry traditional onion with sweet, gentle parsnips. A marriage made in heaven? I think so. (See photo, p. 56)

In a large bowl, mix flaxseeds with 1 ¾ cup (415 mL) water. Let sit for 10 minutes.

In a large pot on high, heat 2 in (5 cm) neutral-flavored oil to 375°F (190°C) on a deep-fry thermometer, or so that a small piece of batter dropped into hot oil immediately sizzles vigorously. Line a plate with paper towels and set aside.

Whisk flours, salt, coriander, turmeric, cayenne, poppy seeds, and black pepper into water and flaxseed mixture to form a thick, smooth batter. Stir in onions and parsnips.

Carefully drop randomly shaped batter by the tablespoonful into hot oil. Cook 4 minutes, until golden brown and crispy, using metal tongs to turn as necessary. Remove from oil using a slotted spoon and drain on paper towels.

Resist the urge to make these uniform — slightly differing sizes and shapes are part of the charm.

Also resist the urge to use more than about 1 ½ tbsp of batter per bhaji, or your bhaji may have uncooked centers — and uncooked chickpea flour is not pleasant.

If not serving each batch immediately as it comes out of the hot oil, heat oven to 200°F (95°C) and place drained bhaji on a plate in oven to keep warm and crisp until you can serve all batches at once.

Makes 24 bhaji

2 tbsp ground flaxseeds

5 cups (1.25 L) neutral-flavored oil for frying
or enough for a depth of 2–3 in (5–8 cm)
in pot

1/4 cup (60 mL) rice flour
1/4 cup (60 mL) chickpea flour
1/4 cup (60 mL) potato flour
1/2 tsp salt
1/2 tsp ground coriander
1/4 tsp turmeric
1/4 tsp cayenne pepper, more to taste
1/4 tsp poppy seeds
1/8 tsp freshly ground black pepper

1 cup (250 mL) thinly sliced onions
1 cup (250 mL) peeled and grated parsnips

Spiced Phyllo Triangles

Fusing flavors found in Middle Eastern cooking with a root found in the tropics, these tasty parcels will be a welcome addition to your table. If you'd prefer to serve these as a main with salad and bread, allow 4–6 per serving.

Makes 24 triangles

Filling

1 1/2 cups (375 mL) peeled and cubed
  tropical yams
1 habañero pepper, scored

2 tbsp olive oil

1 medium onion, finely chopped
2 garlic cloves, minced

1 tsp dried thyme
1/2 tsp ground sumac
1/2 tsp ground cumin
1/2 tsp ground coriander
1/2 tsp salt
1/4 tsp freshly ground black pepper
1/4 tsp ground cardamom
1/4 tsp ground nutmeg
1/4 tsp turmeric
1/8 tsp ground cloves

1 cup (250 mL) cooked green lentils
1 1/3 cups (315 mL) tomato juice

2 cups (500 mL) baby spinach or roughly
  chopped spinach

Prepare filling

Bring a medium saucepan of water to a boil. Add yams and habañero, return water to a boil, and cook for 30 minutes, until yam is tender. Drain and discard cooking water and habañero. Rinse yams under cold water until cool enough to handle, then roughly dice.

In large frying pan on medium, heat 2 tbsp oil. Sauté onions and garlic for 5 minutes, until soft and lightly browned. Add thyme, sumac, cumin, coriander, salt, pepper, cardamom, nutmeg, turmeric, and cloves. Sauté for 30 seconds, until fragrant. Stir in lentils, tomato juice, and yams. Cook, stirring occasionally, until liquid is reduced and thickened, about 10 minutes. Add spinach and cook 2 minutes to wilt completely. Remove from heat and stir in olives and parsley. Allow to cool for 20 minutes.

Preheat oven to 400°F (200°C). Line a large baking sheet with parchment paper.

Prepare pastry

Fill a small bowl with ½ cup oil. Have a pastry brush ready. Unfold phyllo and keep sheets not in use covered with a damp tea towel.

On a clean work surface, lay 1 sheet phyllo. Using pastry brush, brush very lightly with oil, fold in half lengthwise, brush again, and fold in half lengthwise again. You should have a long narrow strip of pastry.

Place 2 tbsp filling at top end of strip. Fold pastry in a triangular fashion over filling, and continue to fold in triangle shape as you move down strip of pastry. Place on tray. Repeat until all filling and pastry are used up. Brush tops of pastries with oil.

Bake for 15–18 minutes, until crispy and golden brown. Check often in the last few minutes, as they can burn quickly.

Substitute an equal weight of cooked white-fleshed sweet potatoes or waxy (such as Fingerling) potatoes for the tropical yam, and skip the yam preparation step.

Yam preparation can be completed in advance and the cooked yam refrigerated for up to 3 days, until required.

These triangles are tasty cold or hot. To reheat, preheat oven to 300°F (150°C) and bake for 10 minutes.

You'll need ⅓ cup (80 mL) green lentils to make 1 cup cooked lentils.

1/4 cup (60 mL) roughly chopped green olives

1/4 cup (60 mL) finely chopped parsley

Pastry
1/2 cup (125 mL) olive oil

24 sheets frozen phyllo dough, thawed per package directions

Sunchoke & Spinach Pakoras

Indian street food made with a native North American root vegetable—true fusion food. The cooking method here is similar to that for Onion & Parsnip Bhaji (p. 59), though these pakoras are not gluten-free.

Makes 24 pakoras

1 tbsp coconut oil

1 medium shallot, finely chopped

1 garlic clove, minced

1 cup (250 mL) scrubbed and grated
    sunchoke

3 cups (750 mL) baby spinach, roughly
    chopped

5 cups (1.25 L) neutral-flavored oil for frying
    or enough for a depth of 2–3 in (5–8 cm)
    in the pot

1 cup (250 mL) all-purpose flour

1 tbsp potato starch

1 tsp baking powder

3/4 tsp ground cumin

1/2 tsp ground fenugreek

1/2 tsp salt

1/4 tsp garlic powder

1/8 tsp freshly ground black pepper

3/4 cup (175 mL) canned coconut milk

In a large frying pan on medium, heat coconut oil. Sauté shallots, garlic, and sunchokes for 5 minutes, until soft. Add spinach and sauté 2–3 minutes, until wilted. Remove from heat and cool for at least 5 minutes.

In a deep fryer or large pot on high, heat 2 in (5 cm) neutral-flavored oil to 375°F (190°C) on a deep-fry thermometer, or so that a small piece of sunchoke dropped into hot oil immediately sizzles vigorously. Line a plate with paper towels and set aside.

In a large bowl, sift flour, potato starch, baking powder, cumin, fenugreek, salt, garlic powder, and black pepper. Make a well. Add coconut milk and 1 cup (250 mL) water to well. Whisk to form a thin batter. Stir in sautéed sunchokes, shallots, and spinach.

Drop scant 1 tbsp measures of batter carefully into oil, taking care not to crowd pot. Cook for 4–5 minutes, turning if required, until golden brown and crisp. Remove with metal tongs or slotted spoon. Drain on paper towel-lined plate.

Don't be tempted to make these too big—they'll be doughy and you'll get fewer gorgeously crunchy bits. Like the bhaji, part of the charm is their random sizes and shapes.

If you haven't used fenugreek before, be warned that it's quite pungent—however, after cooking the taste mellows.

Carrot & White Bean Croquettes

A mild, tasty starter course bursting with fresh carrot and herb flavors. These croquettes can stand alone served with Beet & Balsamic Reduction (p. 168) or paired with a salad for a more substantial starter.

Preheat oven to 400°F (200°C). Line a baking sheet with parchment paper.

In a large bowl, mash beans until only a few larger lumps remain. Stir in cooked quinoa. Set aside.

In a large frying pan on medium, heat oil. Sauté shallots, garlic, and carrots for 8 minutes, until soft, lightly browned, and reduced by two-thirds in volume. Add parsley, thyme, rosemary, salt, sage, and pepper. Sauté for 2 minutes.

Remove from heat and combine with beans and quinoa. Stir in water and chia seeds.

Scoop a scant ⅓ cup (80 mL) mix, and shape into 2-in (5-cm) discs, ½-in (1-cm) high, with your hands. Continue until mix is used up. Place on prepared sheet. Lightly indent each croquette with your thumb.

Bake for 15 minutes, then carefully turn croquettes and bake for 10 more minutes, until firm and both sides are golden.

You can use 1 tsp dried thyme and ¼ tsp dried rosemary in place of fresh herbs, but fresh is better.

Croquettes can be refrigerated for up to 3 days — a perfect make-ahead cheat for a multi-course meal.

Makes 8 croquettes

1 1/2 cups (375 mL) cooked cannellini beans, drained and rinsed
1 cup (250 mL) cooked quinoa (from 1/3 cup [80 mL] uncooked)

1 tbsp olive oil
1 shallot, finely chopped
2 garlic cloves, minced
1 1/4 cups (310 mL) peeled and finely chopped carrots

1/4 cup (60 mL) finely chopped fresh parsley
1 tbsp finely chopped fresh thyme
1 tsp finely chopped fresh rosemary
3/4 tsp salt
1/2 tsp dried sage
1/4 tsp freshly ground black pepper

3 tbsp water
1 tbsp ground chia seeds

➔ *True Facts: Lotus Root*

Lotus root is usually available in Asian grocery stores; it may be sold whole, or pre-peeled, sliced, and vacuum-packed. If it's whole, you just have to peel and slice it yourself.

Place peeled slices immediately in water with a little lemon juice, as lotus root will discolor quickly.

Lotus root cannot be eaten raw, but also does not require cooking in two stages. It will remain crunchy when fully cooked, so don't cook it for longer than the time specified.

Lotus Root Tempura gf

The lightest of batters encases the crispiest slivers of vegetables.
Serve hot with Sesame Horseradish Dipping Sauce (p. 189).

Line a large plate with paper towels.

In a medium bowl, add ½ cup (125 mL) rice flour. Add lotus root slices to flour and toss to lightly coat.

In a large soup pot on medium high, heat oil to 400°F (200°C) on a deep-fry thermometer, or so that a small piece of batter dropped into hot oil immediately sizzles vigorously.

Once oil is hot, in a large bowl whisk together 1 cup rice flour, potato starch, baking powder, salt, coriander, cayenne, and pepper. Make a well and add sparkling water. Whisk to combine. Batter will be thin and fluffy.

Dip floured lotus root slices in batter to coat, then place carefully in hot oil, taking care not to overcrowd pot. Fry for 2–3 minutes, turning as necessary, until lightly golden (tempura will not brown), puffy, and crisp. Drain on paper towels.

For best results, slice lotus root as thinly as possible, no thicker than
¹⁄₁₆ in (1.5 mm), using a mandoline or slicer blade of a food processor.

Makes 4–6 servings

1/2 cup (125 mL) white rice flour

5–6-in (12–15-cm) length lotus root, peeled
and sliced 1/16-in (1.5-mm) thick

5 cups (1.25 L) neutral-flavored oil for frying
or enough for a depth of 2–3 in (5–8 cm)
in the pot

1 cup (250 mL) white rice flour
1 tbsp potato starch
1 tsp baking powder
1/2 tsp salt
1/2 tsp ground coriander
1/8 tsp cayenne
1/8 tsp freshly ground black pepper

1 cup (250 mL) cold sparkling water

Pounded Lime-Taro Breaded Bites

Bursting with the zest of lime, these morsels will get your taste buds dancing—and ready for the next course. Pass around with Spicy Lime Ketchup (recipe below) on the side. (See photo, p. 56)

Makes 12 bites

Spicy Lime Ketchup
1/4 cup (60 mL) ketchup
3 tbsp lime juice
1 1/2 tbsp agave syrup
1/8 tsp chile flakes
1/8 tsp salt

Bites
1 cup (250 mL) peeled and cubed taro

2 tbsp lime juice
1 tbsp finely chopped parsley
1 1/2 tsp lime zest
1/2 tsp salt
1/4 tsp freshly ground black pepper

1/4 cup (60 mL) + 2 tbsp all-purpose flour

1/4 cup (60 mL) panko
1/2 tsp lime zest
1/4 tsp salt
1/8 tsp freshly ground black pepper

3 tbsp olive oil

Prepare taro

Bring a medium saucepan of water to a boil. Add taro, bring water back to a boil, and cook for 30 minutes to ensure taro is perfectly tender. Drain and discard cooking water, and rinse under cold running water.

Make ketchup

In a small bowl, whisk together ketchup, lime juice, syrup, chile flakes and salt. Set aside.

Make bites

In a large bowl, mash cooled taro until smooth. Add lime juice, parsley, lime zest, salt, and pepper. Stir to combine. Mix in flour. Form into tablespoon-sized balls and flatten each to 1-in (2.5-cm) diameter discs.

In a small bowl, mix panko, lime zest, salt, and pepper to create breading mixture. Coat discs in breading mixture.

In a large frying pan on medium-high, heat oil. Fry in batches, taking care not to crowd pan, for 1–2 minutes per side, until golden brown.

See information (p. 35) about working with taro.

Baked Beet Cakes gf

Gently spiced to enhance beets' natural sweetness, these cakes taste great hot or at room temperature. Plate with a salad, or serve as a finger food appetizer lightly dotted with vegan sour cream and parsley or decorated with a thin slice of cucumber or tomato.

Preheat oven to 400°F (200°C). Line a baking sheet with parchment paper and lightly apply non-stick spray.

In a large pot, add water to just cover sweet potato cubes, grated beets, and grated parsnips. Cover and bring to a boil, then reduce heat to medium-low and simmer, uncovered, until sweet potatoes are very tender, about 15 minutes.

Drain and mash until mixture is smooth. Allow to cool for 10 minutes. (Recipe can be made in advance to this point. Refrigerate until ready to use and bring to room temperature before proceeding.)

Add remaining ingredients to mixture, and combine well. Mix should hold together, but if it's too dry, add a little water. Measure generous tablespoon-sized scoops, and with your hands shape into neat 2-in (5-cm) discs.

Place on baking sheet 1 in (2.5 cm) apart (cakes don't spread) and bake for 30 minutes, turning halfway through baking time.

These beet cakes also make a cute side dish.

Cook beets, sweet potatoes, and parsnips in advance, mash, and refrigerate until required. Bring to room temperature before continuing.

Make beet cakes and refrigerate until ready to bake. You can even bake these in advance and reheat at 300°F (150°C) for 10 minutes.

Instead of baking, you can fry the beet cakes in a non-stick frying pan with a little non-stick spray, until golden on each side, about 10 minutes in total.

Makes 22 cakes

1 cup (250 mL) peeled and cubed sweet potatoes, orange- or white-fleshed

2 cups (500 mL) peeled and grated beets

1 cup (250 mL) peeled and grated parsnips

3/4 cup (175 mL) quick-cooking rolled oats (not instant)

1 finely chopped shallot

2 garlic cloves, minced

1 chipotle in adobo, seeded and finely chopped

1 tsp salt, or to taste

1/4 tsp ground white pepper

1/2 tsp smoked paprika

1/8 tsp ground fennel seeds

Sesame Sweet Potato Spinach Sushi

A little combo roll you're not likely to see elsewhere—a shame because it looks pretty and tastes of intense sesame and hits of sour—along with chewy rice and seaweed.

Makes 15–18 pieces

1 cup (250 mL) white sushi rice
1 1/2 cups (375 mL) water
pinch salt

2 tbsp unseasoned rice vinegar
1/2 tbsp brown rice syrup

1/2 tbsp black sesame seeds
1/2 tbsp sesame oil
1/2 tbsp soy sauce

1 tbsp ume plum vinegar or rice wine
  vinegar
1/2 tbsp white sesame seeds

1/2 small orange-fleshed sweet potato
  peeled and cut into 2-in (5-cm) long,
  1/8-in (3-mm) wide slices

4 cups (1 L) baby spinach leaves

2 1/2 tbsp white sesame seeds
2 1/2 tbsp black sesame seeds

3 toasted nori sheets, 8-in (20-cm) square

Rinse rice and place in a medium saucepan. Cover with 1 ½ cups (375 mL) water and add salt. Bring to a boil, reduce heat to medium-low, cover, and cook for 15 minutes. Remove from heat and let sit for 5 minutes.

Transfer rice to large non-metallic bowl. Add vinegar and syrup, stirring for 1 minute with a wide non-metallic spoon or spatula in one hand, while fanning with the other hand to help cool the rice. Leave in bowl and stir occasionally as you prepare fillings.

In a medium bowl, combine black sesame seeds, sesame oil, and soy sauce.

In a small bowl, combine ume plum vinegar and white sesame seeds.

Bring a medium saucepan of water to a boil. Add sweet potato pieces and cook for 8 minutes, until tender. Using a slotted spoon, remove sweet potatoes and rinse under cold water to cool. Add to bowl with black sesame seeds and toss to coat.

Add spinach to sweet potato water in saucepan and cook for 30 seconds to just wilt. Drain and rinse with cold water to cool. Squeeze out excess water. Add to small bowl with ume vinegar and mix well.

Place black and white sesame seeds (for garnish) on large rimmed plate or in shallow bowl.

Place a sushi mat on your workstation. Line with plastic wrap cut to the same size as mat.

Place 1 cup (250 mL) rice on plastic wrap. Using wet hands, press into a thin layer 8-in (20-cm) square (smaller than the mat). Cover rice completely with 1 sheet toasted nori. Place one-third of sweet potatoes in a 2-in (5-cm) wide strip along edge of nori closest to you. Place one-third of spinach along center of strip of sweet potatoes.

Roll carefully away from you, using mat and plastic wrap as a guide. Press on the roll as you go, removing plastic wrap as you roll. Once rolled, press gently to seal, and remove plastic wrap.

Roll sushi roll in seeds on plate so they adhere to the rice on the outside of the roll.

Using a serrated knife, slice roll into 6 equal-sized pieces. Larger slices are difficult to eat; smaller slices are likely to fall apart as you cut. Serve at room temperature.

The next time you're in your local sushi place or a supermarket with a sushi bar, take a few minutes to watch professionals roll sushi. It'll help you see how to roll your own.

Black sesame seeds are often found in the spice aisle. You can use only white sesame seeds — the sushi won't look as intense but will still have the taste and textural impact.

Fresh Spring Rolls with Daikon

There's a learning curve to making fresh spring rolls with rice paper wrappers—so don't get discouraged if the first attempts look less than perfect, as mine often do. Serve with Carrot Peanut Sauce (p. 185) or the Sesame Horseradish Dipping Sauce (p. 189, for a raw option, don't toast the seeds) for some more zing.

Makes 8 spring rolls

1/2 tbsp lime juice

1/2 tbsp agave syrup

1/4 tsp ground cumin

1/8 tsp chile flakes

1/8 tsp paprika

pinch salt

2-in (5-cm) length daikon, grated

8 sheets rice paper spring roll wrappers

16 soft lettuce leaves, such as Bibb or Boston

1/2 cup (125 mL) finely grated carrots

1/4 cup (60 mL) cilantro leaves

1/4 cup (60 mL) raw peanuts, roughly chopped

1 avocado, sliced into 16 slices

In a small bowl, stir together lime juice, agave syrup, ground cumin, chile flakes, paprika, and salt. Mix in grated daikon. Let sit to develop flavor while preparing other vegetables.

Assemble spring rolls

Set up a workstation with individual ingredients in small bowls arranged within reach.

Fill a large, straight-sided sauté pan with hot tap water and put to one side of workstation. Beside it, place a clean tea towel to absorb excess water from rice paper wrappers.

Submerge 1 rice paper wrapper in hot water for 30 seconds, until just pliable. Transfer to clean tea towel.

Place 2 soft lettuce leaves on rice paper wrapper, away from edges and slightly off-center. Top with 2 tbsp seasoned daikon, 1 tbsp grated carrots, ½ tbsp cilantro leaves, ½ tbsp raw peanuts, and 2 slices avocado.

Fold sides of wrapper toward the center and hold them down gently with your fingers while using your thumbs to lift and fold the part of the wrapper closest to you up and over the fillings. Roll wrapper away from you, keeping it firm and tight. The wrapper will seal itself.

Place completed spring roll on serving platter. Continue until wrappers and fillings are used up.

Truly Comforting Soups

Smooth and creamy, thick and soothing, light and refreshing— this chapter really has it all. Flavor profiles run the gauntlet from Europe to Asia and back in new fusion soups, as well as more traditional ones.

Drunken Turnip Soup *gf* option

This smooth, beer-laden, rich and creamy split pea soup pops with boozy, smoke-infused turnip pieces. (See photo, p. 76)

In a large soup pot on medium-high, heat oil. Add turnips and sauté for 3–4 minutes, until golden brown. Add leeks and sauté for 2–3 minutes to soften and lightly brown. Remove from heat and stir in liquid smoke and whiskey. Transfer to a bowl and set aside.

In same pot on medium, heat oil and sauté shallots, carrots, and potatoes for 5 minutes, until softened and starting to brown. Add split peas, beer, stock, and bay leaf. Stir and increase heat to bring to a boil. Once it boils, reduce heat to medium-low, cover, and simmer for 45–50 minutes, until split peas and vegetables are completely tender. Remove bay leaf.

Using an immersion blender, or in a countertop blender, working in batches, purée until soup is smooth and creamy. Return to pot. Taste and season as desired.

Add turnip mixture to soup. Heat on medium for 5 minutes to combine flavors and warm turnip pieces through.

If you like a more rustic look, don't blend the soup before adding the turnips.

Makes 2–4 servings

2 tsp coconut oil
1 1/2 cups (375 mL) peeled and diced turnips

1 1/2 cups (375 mL) finely chopped leeks, white and light green leaves only

1 1/2 tsp liquid smoke
3 tbsp whiskey

2 tsp coconut oil
1 medium shallot, finely chopped
1 cup (250 mL) peeled and finely chopped carrots
1 cup (250 mL) peeled and finely chopped potatoes

3/4 cup (175 mL) green split peas
1 3/4 cups (415 mL) beer, preferably a medium-bodied lager (or gluten-free beer or vegetable stock)
3 cups (750 mL) vegetable stock
1 bay leaf

salt and freshly ground black pepper, to taste

Purple Potato & Caramelized Onion Soup

Puréed purple potatoes look beautifully velvety in the bowl, but they taste just like yellow potatoes, so you can use Yukon Gold instead. Caramelizing the onions takes bit of time, but the flavor is worth it. Serve hot or cold as you would a vichyssoise.

In a large pot on medium, heat oil. Add onions and salt. Cook, covered, stirring occasionally and more frequently toward the end of cooking time, until very soft, golden brown, and reduced by a quarter in volume, about 45 minutes.

Add caraway seeds and garlic. Sauté for 1 minute, then deglaze pot with wine.

Stir in grated potatoes, then add stock, thyme, bay leaf, and salt. Bring to a boil, reduce heat to medium-low, and simmer, uncovered, for 20 minutes, until potatoes are tender. Remove bay leaf and thyme sprig.

Using an immersion blender, or countertop blender in batches, purée soup until completely smooth. Stir in lemon juice. Taste and adjust seasonings as desired.

Garnish each bowl with ¼ tsp fresh thyme leaves.

If you'd like to add a little texture, serve crackers or breadsticks with this smooth soup, or sprinkle with Potato Croutons (p. 99).

Makes 4 servings

1 tbsp olive oil

1 large or 2 medium sweet onions, such as Vidalia or Walla Walla, quartered and thinly sliced

pinch salt

1/2 tsp caraway seeds

2 garlic cloves, minced

1/4 cup (60 mL) white wine, such as sauvignon blanc

3 cups (750 mL) scrubbed and grated purple or Yukon Gold potatoes (peeling optional)

5 1/2 cups (1.3 L) vegetable or onion stock

sprig fresh thyme

1 bay leaf

1/2 tsp salt

1 tsp lemon juice

1 tsp fresh thyme leaves to garnish

↪ *Roast Those Roots*

Follow these tips to roast any root vegetable with ease.

- Ensure the oven is hot for quick cooking and caramelizing. Preheat oven to 425°F (220°C) while you prepare the vegetables. Line a roasting pan with parchment paper for easier cleanup.

- In large mixing bowl, combine the cut roots to be roasted with a small amount (start with 1 tbsp) of neutral-flavored oil or oil of choice, a pinch of salt and pepper, and any other herbs or spices that take your fancy. Toss to coat and spread on roasting pan in single layer.

- If roasting just one type of vegetable, cut uniform pieces. Bite-sized are best for quick cooking, which takes approximately 20–30 minutes. Larger pieces may take 45 minutes to reach tender crispness.

- If roasting a mix of vegetables, cut denser roots, such as parsnips, beets, or carrots, into smaller pieces as they will take longer to cook. Or place in oven for 10 minutes, and then add the less dense vegetables, such as sweet potatoes.

- Use a large roasting pan so vegetables will not be overcrowded (otherwise, they will steam, not roast).

- Remove pan from oven after 15 minutes and toss roots. Repeat every 15 minutes.

- To reduce roasting time, larger pieces of vegetables can be blanched, then drained and dried, before roasting in oven.

Patatas Bravas Soup gf

The traditional Spanish tapa turned on its head. This soup captures the essence of the spicy tomato sauce usually served with crispy fried potatoes. Here, they're used as the garnish. Try not to eat all the potatoes out of the pan before they get to the soup.

Preheat oven to 425°F (220°C). Line a baking sheet with parchment paper.

In a large pot on medium, heat 1 tbsp oil. Sauté bell peppers, shallots, and garlic for 5 minutes, until soft and starting to brown. Add paprika, cayenne, salt, and black pepper, and sauté for 30 seconds.

Stir in tomato paste, canned tomatoes, vegetable stock, vinegar and syrup. Bring to a boil, then reduce heat to medium-low and simmer, uncovered, until soup is thickened and a rich red color, about 35–40 minutes.

While soup cooks, in a large bowl, mix together oil, parsley, yeast, salt, paprika, and oregano. Add potatoes and toss to coat. Spread in a single layer on prepared baking sheet.

Bake for 10 minutes, until just tender. Remove from oven, toss potatoes, and bake for 10–12 more minutes, until golden brown and crispy. Remove from oven and set aside.

Using an immersion or countertop blender, blend soup to desired consistency (be careful when handling hot liquids). Ladle into serving bowls and evenly divide potato garnish among bowls. Sprinkle with fresh parsley.

Blend to preference. I like some texture with enough body to support the potato garnish.

Makes 2–4 servings

Soup

1 tbsp olive oil

1 red bell pepper, finely chopped

2 shallots, finely chopped,

1 garlic clove, minced

1 tsp smoked paprika

1 tsp Spanish or regular paprika

1/8–1/4 tsp cayenne, to taste (optional)

1/2 tsp salt

1/4 tsp freshly ground black pepper

1/4 cup (60 mL) tomato paste

2 1/2 cups (625 mL) canned diced tomatoes

2 1/2 cups (625 mL) vegetable stock

1 tbsp red wine vinegar

1 tsp brown rice syrup

Crispy Potato Garnish

2 tbsp olive oil

2 tbsp finely chopped fresh parsley

2 tsp nutritional yeast

1 tsp salt

1 tsp smoked paprika

1/2 tsp dried oregano

3 Yukon Gold potatoes, peeled and diced

2 tbsp finely chopped fresh parsley

Golden Borscht gf

The milder cousin to traditional red borscht, this version is sweeter, less earthy, and lightly accented with herbs—nothing too punchy or intense. Blend the soup to your textural preference—if you like borscht with lots of bits, don't blend; if you like smooth soups, blend all the way to luscious and silky.

Makes 2–4 servings

1 tbsp olive oil

1 medium onion, quartered and thinly sliced

1 1/2 cups (375 mL) cooked chickpeas, roughly mashed

2 celery stalks, thinly sliced

1 medium white or Yukon Gold potato, grated

3 medium golden beets, peeled and grated

2 sprigs fresh thyme

1 tsp salt

2 cups (500 mL) vegetable stock

1/2 cup (125 mL) unsweetened nondairy milk

salt and pepper, to taste

In a large pot on medium-low, heat oil. Add onions, chickpeas, celery, potatoes, beets, thyme, and salt. Stir to combine well.

Cover and cook, stirring often, for 20 minutes, until soft, thick, and reduced by half in volume. If mixture sticks, reduce heat, scrape off burnt bits, and stir them in. Stir in vegetable stock and bring to a boil. Cover and cook on medium-low for 20 minutes, until vegetables are very tender, almost falling apart. Remove from heat. Remove and discard thyme sprigs.

Remove half the soup. Using an immersion blender or in a countertop blender, purée until smooth or desired consistency, and return to pot. Stir in milk and reheat gently for 2–3 minutes. Taste and adjust seasoning as desired.

Spinach, Parsley & Parsnip Soup *gf*

Vibrantly green and bursting with fresh flavors, this light and satisfying soup is great served hot or chilled for a refreshing lunch.

In a large pot on medium, heat oil. Sauté parsnips, parsley stalks, and shallots for 5 minutes, until very soft and lightly browned. Deglaze pot with white wine, stirring for about 1 minute. Stir in potato and both types of parsley leaves.

Add stock and bay leaf. Bring to a boil, reduce heat to medium-low, and simmer for 15 minutes, until potatoes and parsnips are very tender. Add spinach and cook for 2 minutes, so spinach wilts but remains bright green. Remove bay leaf. Stir in lemon juice.

Using an immersion blender, or in a countertop blender, working in batches, purée until soup is smooth and silky.

Makes 2–4 servings

1 tbsp olive oil

1 medium parsnip, scrubbed and finely chopped
2 tbsp parsley stalks, finely chopped
1 shallot, minced

1/2 cup (125 mL) white wine, such as sauvignon blanc

1 medium white or Yukon Gold potato, peeled and finely chopped
1/3 cup (80 mL) flat-leaf parsley leaves
1/3 cup (80 mL) curly parsley leaves

4 cups (1 L) vegetable stock
1 bay leaf

4 cups (1 L) baby spinach

1 tbsp lemon juice

Roasted Carrot & Lentil Soup

Thick, almost reminiscent of dal, this soup is naturally sweet with roasted carrots and spices. If you like a thinner soup, add more stock.

Makes 4 servings

1 tbsp olive oil

5 cups (1.25 L) peeled and roughly chopped
  carrots

1/2 tsp dried thyme

1/2 tsp crumbled dried sage

1/2 tsp dried oregano

salt and freshly ground black pepper, to
  taste

1/4 cup (60 mL) white wine, such as
  sauvignon blanc

1 tbsp olive oil

1 medium onion, finely chopped

3 garlic cloves, minced

1/2 tsp crumbled dried sage

1/2 tsp dried oregano

1/2 tsp dried marjoram

1/4 tsp freshly ground black pepper

1 tsp molasses

1 tsp maple syrup

1 cup (250 mL) red lentils

5 cups (1.25 L) vegetable stock

salt and freshly ground black pepper, to
  taste

Preheat oven to 425°F (220°C).

In a large roasting pan, toss together 1 tbsp oil, carrots, thyme, sage, oregano, salt, and pepper. Roast for 30 minutes, until tender and lightly caramelized. Deglaze roasting pan with wine. (This step can be completed in advance if desired.)

In a large pot on medium, heat 1 tbsp oil and sauté onions for 5 minutes, until translucent. Add garlic, sage, oregano, marjoram, and pepper, and sauté for 1 minute. Stir in molasses, maple syrup, red lentils, and stock. Add roasted carrots and wine. Bring to a boil, then reduce heat to low, cover, and simmer for 30 minutes, until lentils and carrots are very tender.

Using an immersion blender, or in a countertop blender, working in batches, blend until carrots are broken up, but soup is not completely smooth, adding additional stock for a thinner soup. Taste and adjust seasoning as desired.

Curried Sunchoke & Yellow Split Pea Soup

Warming rather than spicy, this soup is perfect for a wet fall day. Roasted garlic adds subliminal richness; it's worth taking the time for that extra step. It may seem like the recipe calls for a lot of liquid, but remember this soup cooks for a long time. The peas will absorb much of the liquid and thicken the soup.

Preheat oven to 425°F (220°C). Slice top off each head of garlic, drizzle with 1 tsp oil, wrap in aluminum foil, and roast for 25 minutes, until very soft. Remove from oven, unwrap, and let cool.

In a large pot on medium, heat 1 tbsp oil. Sauté onions for 5 minutes until soft and translucent. Add curry powder, cumin, garlic powder, coriander, cardamom, salt, and pepper. Sauté for 30 seconds.

Squeeze roasted garlic from skins into pot. Add tomato paste, sunchokes, and split peas. Sauté for 1 minute to coat sunchokes and split peas with spices.

Add stock and bay leaf. Bring to a boil, then reduce heat to medium-low, partially cover, and simmer for 60–65 minutes, until sunchokes and split peas are tender and falling apart. Remove bay leaf.

Using an immersion blender, or in a countertop blender, working in batches, blend until smooth. Add additional liquid if required. Taste and adjust seasoning as desired.

Makes 2–4 servings

2 heads garlic, papery skins removed
1 tsp + 1 tbsp olive oil

1 tbsp olive oil
1 medium onion, finely chopped

2 tsp medium curry powder
1/2 tsp ground cumin
1/2 tsp garlic powder
1/2 tsp ground coriander
1/4 tsp ground cardamom
1/2 tsp salt
1/8 tsp freshly ground black pepper

1/2 tbsp tomato paste
3 medium sunchokes, peeled and roughly chopped
3/4 cup (175 mL) yellow split peas

6 1/2 cups (1.63 L) vegetable stock
1 bay leaf

salt and freshly ground black pepper to taste

Leek & Sweet Potato Soup *gf*

Very simply spiced, this soup really lets the natural flavors of the vegetables shine. It's a sweeter and heartier version of traditional vichyssoise, and like the original can be served hot or cold. When served hot, I leave it chunky, but when serving it cold, I like it super smooth. I'll even pass it through a sieve to get the smoothest texture I can.

Makes 4 servings

1 tbsp olive oil

1/2 tsp celery seed

1/4 cup (60 mL) finely chopped spring onions, light green and white parts only, darker green leaves reserved for garnish

1/2 cup (125 mL) finely chopped celery

2 1/2–3 cups (625 to 750 mL) cleaned, trimmed, and finely sliced leeks

2 lb (1 kg) sweet potatoes, white- or orange-fleshed, peeled and diced

1/3 cup (80 mL) red lentils

5 cups (1.25 L) vegetable stock

salt and freshly ground black pepper to taste

In a large pot on medium-high, heat oil. Add seeds and allow to sizzle, about 1 minute. Add spring onions, celery, and leeks. Sauté for 3–5 minutes, until soft and lightly browned in places. Add sweet potatoes and lentils, toss to coat, then add stock.

Cover pot, bring to a boil, then reduce heat to medium-low, and simmer for 15–20 minutes, until potatoes and lentils are tender.

Using an immersion blender, or in a countertop blender, working in batches, blend to your preferred consistency. Taste and adjust seasoning as desired. Serve hot or let cool and chill before serving.

Radish & Red Quinoa Soup gf

A warm, comforting broth full of protein-rich quinoa and flavorful vegetables enveloping hidden gems of barely cooked radish—all topped with an herby crunch.

In a blender or food processor, pulse together radish greens, cilantro leaves, pumpkin seeds, 1 tbsp oil, salt, cumin, and chile flakes until well combined and broken up but not smooth. Transfer to a small bowl and refrigerate while making soup.

In a large pot on medium-high, heat 1 tbsp oil. Add cumin seeds and cilantro stalks and allow to sizzle for 1 minute. Add shallots and jalapeño and sauté for 2 minutes, until soft and fragrant. Add carrots, celery, potatoes, and quinoa. Sauté for 5 minutes, until vegetables are softened. Add stock and cook for 15 minutes, until quinoa and vegetables are cooked. Remove from heat. Stir in thinly sliced radishes.

Ladle into serving bowls and top with prepared garnish.

You can use white quinoa, but red is sturdier and holds its shape better—it also looks pretty with the red radishes.

Makes 2–4 servings

Herb Crunch
1/2 cup (125 mL) radish greens
1/4 cup (60 mL) cilantro leaves
1/4 cup (60 mL) pumpkin seeds
1 tbsp olive oil
1/8 tsp salt
1/8 tsp ground cumin
1/8 tsp chile flakes

Soup
1 tbsp olive oil
1/2 tsp cumin seeds
2 tbsp finely chopped cilantro stalks

1 shallot, finely chopped
1 jalapeño or serrano pepper, finely
  chopped (seeding optional)

1/2 cup (125 mL) peeled and finely chopped
  carrots
1/2 cup (125 mL) trimmed and finely
  chopped celery
1/2 cup (125 mL) scrubbed and finely
  chopped red-skinned potatoes
3/4 cup (175 mL) red quinoa

5 cups (1.25 L) vegetable stock

12 radishes, trimmed, halved and sliced into
  1/8-in (3-mm) rounds

Caribbean Taro & Plantain Black Bean Soup

Flavors of the Caribbean elevate the neutral tastes of taro and plantain to something spectacular. Black beans provide rich color and a great hit of protein.

Makes 2 servings

3/4 cup (175 mL) peeled and cubed taro

2 cups (500 mL) neutral-flavored oil or enough for a depth of 2 in (5 cm) in a small saucepan

1 medium green plantain, peeled and cubed
pinch salt

1 tbsp coconut oil
1/3 cup (80 mL) thinly sliced spring onions

1 1/2 cups (375 mL) cooked black beans, drained and rinsed
1/4 tsp ground allspice
1/4 tsp salt
1/8 tsp ground nutmeg

1 cup (250 mL) coconut milk
2 cups (500 mL) vegetable stock
1 habañero pepper, scored 4 times
1 cinnamon stick
1 thyme sprig
1 bay leaf

1 tbsp freshly squeezed lime juice

Prepare taro

Bring a medium saucepan of water to a boil. Add taro and return water to a boil. Cook for 12 minutes to ensure taro is tender. Drain and discard cooking water. (This step can be completed in advance.)

Prepare plantain

In a medium saucepan on medium-high, heat oil to 375°F (190°C) on a deep-fry thermometer, or so that a small piece of plantain sizzles immediately. Line a plate with paper towels.

Fry plantain pieces for 2 minutes, until golden brown. Work in batches and don't overcrowd the pan, Drain plantain on paper towels.

Place half the plantain with cooked taro. (This step can be completed in advance.)

Using a fork, squish remaining plantain pieces into flat discs, then fry for 2 minutes, until crispy and brown.

Drain on paper towels and sprinkle with salt while still hot. Place twice-fried plantain pieces to one side for a garnish.

Prepare soup

In a large pot on medium, heat oil. Sauté spring onions for 1–2 minutes, until soft. Add cooked taro, once-cooked plantain, black beans, allspice, salt, and nutmeg. Sauté for 2 minutes.

Add coconut milk, stock, habañero, cinnamon stick, thyme, and bay leaf. Bring to a boil, reduce heat to medium-low, and simmer, partially covered, for 20–25 minutes, until taro falls apart when pierced and plantain is very tender. Remove habañero, cinnamon stick, thyme stalk, and bay leaf.

Using an immersion blender, or in a countertop blender, working in batches, blend soup to preferred consistency, keeping some texture or blending until smooth. Stir in lime juice. Taste and adjust seasoning as desired. Garnish with fried plantain slices.

Don't be scared of the habañero. Scoring and cooking it in broth infuses the soup with the pepper's wonderful fruity intensity and only a small fraction of its heat. Remove the pepper before blending, unless you're a heat lover.

For information about using taro, see textbox (p. 35).

What I call tropical yams are true yams (botanically speaking, genus *Dioscorea*), not the orange-fleshed sweet potatoes known in North America as yams (genus *Ipomoea*), or the small, knobby, orange-pink tubers (genus *Oxalis*) known in New Zealand as New Zealand yams.

True or tropical yams are formed on the roots of vine-like plants native to Africa, Asia, Latin America, and the Caribbean. There are many edible varieties within this family, and they tend to be both drier and starchier than sweet potatoes.

Many varieties of yam are toxic if eaten raw and must be properly and completely cooked before eating. To be on the safe side, tropical yams are cooked twice—first boiled to tenderness, then cooked again with the dish to add flavor. Do not skip the initial boiling step— please err on the side of caution.

I've seen tropical yams sold under the names yam, fresh yam, and Caribbean yam. Japanese yams or Nagaimo roots, which are sold in Asian stores, are a part of this family and will also work in these recipes. If you cannot locate a true yam, use the same weight of white-fleshed sweet potatoes instead, and skip the pre-cooking step.

Yuca must never be eaten raw. In my recipes it's cooked twice—first, boiled to tenderness, then cooked again to add flavor. Do not skip the initial boiling step thinking you can cook it longer during the second step—yuca can be poisonous if not fully cooked, so please err on the side of caution.

Frozen yuca can be used in place of fresh—look for it in Asian stores or those selling Latin American foods. It still needs to be pre-cooked, and it can be cooked from frozen; just check for tenderness and add more time if necessary.

The hard, woody, fibrous center, like a hard string, should not be eaten. It's easier to find and remove after the yuca has been boiled; however, it can be removed from the final dish as you would remove a clove or bay leaf. Just don't eat it.

Fresh yuca has a thick skin that's usually covered with a waxy preservative. The entire skin, including the thin, red-tinged inner skin, needs to be removed and discarded. Cut the root into manageable lengths of 3 in (8 cm) or so, place upright on a cutting board, and run a sharp paring knife down the length to remove the skin.

Cut yuca discolors quickly, so place cut pieces in water with 1 tbsp lemon or lime juice.

Eating unseasoned yuca is like eating pure starch; seasoning transforms it into the most delectable taste sensation.

Yuca & Tropical Yam Peanut Soup

Rich and comforting, each bowl of this soup transports you to sub-Saharan Africa.

Prepare yuca and yam

Bring a medium saucepan of water to a boil. Add yuca and yam and return water to a boil. Cook for 15 minutes to ensure vegetables are cooked and tender. Drain and discard cooking water. Rinse under cold water to cool and set aside.

Prepare soup

In a large measuring cup or medium mixing bowl, stir together coconut milk and peanut butter to emulsify. Set aside.

In a large pot on medium, heat oil. Sauté onions, celery and bell peppers for 5 minutes, until soft and lightly browned. Add red chile, ginger, and garlic. Sauté for 30 seconds. Add yuca and yam pieces. Sauté for 1 minute to coat with spices.

Add stock, bring to a boil, reduce heat to medium-low, and cook for 15–20 minutes, until yuca and yam are falling apart.

Stir 1 cup (250 mL) liquid from soup into peanut butter/coconut milk mixture, then add mixture to pot and stir to combine. This helps to prevent mixture from curdling. Add spinach and salt and cook for 2 minutes, until just wilted. Taste and adjust seasoning as desired. Garnish each bowl with 1 tbsp roasted peanuts.

If making ahead, reheat gently on low. Do not boil again once peanut butter mix has been stirred in.

For hints on using yuca and tropical yams, see p. 88.

Makes 4 servings

1 lb (500 g) yuca, peeled and cubed
8 oz (230 g) tropical yam, peeled and diced

1 cup (250 mL) canned coconut milk
1/2 cup (125 mL) smooth peanut butter

1 tbsp coconut oil

1 medium onion, finely chopped
1 celery stalk, finely chopped
1/2 red bell pepper, seeded and finely chopped
1/2 green bell pepper, seeded and finely chopped

1–2 small red chiles, seeded and minced
1 tbsp grated fresh ginger
1 garlic clove, minced

3 cups (750 mL) vegetable stock

5 packed cups (1.25 L) roughly chopped or baby spinach
1/2 tsp salt

1/4 cup (60 mL) roasted peanuts

Burdock Miso Noodle Soup with Lotus Root Chips *gf* option

Slippery and slurpable, this warming, savory, aromatic broth complements the tender noodles and crunchy burdock. Perfect for lunch or a light supper on a cool day.

Make chips

Preheat oven to 300°F (150°C). Place cooling rack on a large baking sheet to allow air to circulate under chips as they bake.

Using a mandoline or very sharp knife, thinly slice lotus root into less than 1/16-in (1.5-mm) chips. Place on prepared rack.

Bake for 15 minutes, carefully turn chips, and bake for 12–15 minutes, until firm and crispy golden brown.

Make soup

In a small bowl, place lime juice. Peel burdock and slice into thin matchsticks about 1 ½ in (4 cm) long, placing each one in bowl with lime juice as it's cut. Toss to coat.

In a large saucepan on medium-high, heat sesame oil. Drain burdock, add to pan, and sauté for 2 minutes until lightly browned. Add garlic, spring onions, ginger, and cilantro stems, and sauté for 30 seconds, until fragrant.

Add stock and 5 cups water, and bring to a boil. Add noodles, reduce heat to medium, and cook for 8–10 minutes, until noodles are tender. Remove from heat.

In a small bowl, combine ½ cup (125 mL) soup liquid with miso paste. Stir briskly to dissolve, then return to pan and stir to combine.

Divide soup between serving bowls. Sprinkle each bowl with 1 tbsp sliced dark green spring onions and 1 tbsp cilantro leaves. Garnish each bowl with Lotus Root Chips.

I have made this soup with udon, soba, and rice noodles, and each gives a slightly different flavor and texture to the finished soup. Use the noodles you prefer or can most easily find.

Lotus root chips provide a great textural contrast and visual impression, but the soup is great without them.

Makes 2 servings

Lotus Root Chips
1-in (2.5-cm) length lotus root, peeled

Soup
1 tbsp lime juice
9-in (23-cm) length burdock

1 tsp sesame oil

1 garlic clove, minced
2 spring onions, thinly sliced, 2 tbsp green ends reserved for garnish
1 tsp grated fresh ginger
1 tsp minced cilantro stems

1 cup (250 mL) vegetable stock

2 bundles, 8 oz (230 g), udon, soba, or rice noodles

2 tbsp light miso paste
2 tbsp cilantro leaves

➙ True Facts: Burdock

You'll most commonly find burdock in Asian grocery stores. Often sold as long uncut roots, burdock is sometimes packaged in shorter, more manageable lengths.

You may see burdock sold as gobō, its Japanese name.

Burdock discolors very quickly once peeled. To prevent browning, place in water with a little lemon or lime juice as you cut it.

↪ *True Facts: Water Chestnuts*

Native to China, these underwater corms retain their crunch when fully cooked, adding textural contrast to any dish. If fresh water chestnuts are not available in your area, canned pre-peeled chestnuts in water make an acceptable substitute. To peel fresh water chestnuts, slice off the top and bottom, then cut down and around to remove the shells.

Water Chestnut Hot & Sour Soup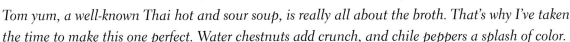

Tom yum, a well-known Thai hot and sour soup, is really all about the broth. That's why I've taken the time to make this one perfect. Water chestnuts add crunch, and chile peppers a splash of color.

In a large pot, combine 4 cups (1 L) water, stock, lemongrass, garlic, ginger discs, lime peel, lime juice, chile peppers, soy sauce, cilantro stems, and syrup. Bring to a boil, reduce heat to medium-low, and simmer for 15 minutes, until herbs and spices are soft.

Using a slotted spoon, scoop aromatics from broth, squeezing their liquid back into the broth, and discard. Add water chestnut slices, mushrooms, and red bell peppers to broth. Simmer for 2 minutes, until heated through. Remove from heat, and stir in cilantro leaves and spring onions to just wilt.

Divide into serving bowls and garnish with chopped peanuts.

Makes 2–4 servings

1 cup (250 mL) vegetable stock

2 lemongrass stalks, trimmed and crushed

2 garlic cloves, peeled and crushed

1-in (2.5-cm) length fresh ginger, sliced into thin discs

zest of 1 lime

3 tbsp lime juice

2 small red (such as bird's eye) chile peppers, scored

2 tbsp soy sauce

1/4 cup (60 mL) cilantro stems

1 tsp brown rice syrup

3/4 cup (175 mL) peeled and sliced water chestnuts, no thicker than 1/16 in (1.5 mm)

1/2 cup (125 mL) enoki, straw, or oyster mushrooms, or a combination, oyster and straw mushrooms sliced, enoki ends trimmed

1/4 cup (60 mL) thinly sliced red bell peppers

1/4 cup (60 mL) cilantro leaves

2 spring onions, sliced thinly on the bias

1/4 cup (60 mL) roasted peanuts, roughly chopped

Truly Innovative Salads

Cooked and cooled or raw—any salad from this selection will be harmonious on your table. Perfect any time of the year, these dressings and seasonings showcase the versatility of root vegetables.

Arugula & Avocado Caesar Salad with Potato Croutons gf

The sharpness of arugula is enhanced by a slightly tart dressing and tempered by smooth avocado and crunchy potato bits. (See photo of croutons, p. 76)

Make dressing

In a blender combine all ingredients and blend until smooth. Taste and season with salt, pepper, or caper brine as desired, blending again with each addition. Refrigerate until required.

Make croutons

Place a large, clean tea towel on a large plate. Line a second large plate with paper towels.

Fit a large pot with a steamer basket. Add 1 cup (250 mL) water to pot.

Cut potatoes into ¼-in (6-mm) dice and place in steamer basket. Bring water to a boil and steam potatoes for 8–9 minutes, until just tender.

Drain potatoes and rinse under cold running water for 1–2 minutes, until cooled to room temperature. Place on clean tea towel and pat dry. Allow to remain on tea towel for 5 minutes to fully dry.

In a small mixing bowl, combine salt, seasoning blend, black pepper, and celery salt.

In a large frying pan on high, heat oil until a piece of potato dropped in sizzles immediately. Add potato pieces and cook for 5–6 minutes, stirring frequently, until golden and crisp. Immediately transfer to bowl with seasoning mixture. Toss to coat evenly, then remove and let drain on paper towels.

Make salad

In a large bowl, toss lettuce, arugula, and spring onions in dressing. Arrange on two large plates and top with diced avocados and croutons.

Makes 2 servings (as a main)

Caesar Dressing

1/2 cup (125 mL) silken tofu

2 garlic cloves, minced

3 tbsp flaxseed oil

2 tbsp capers in brine

2 tbsp sliced green olives

1 tbsp rice vinegar

1 tbsp lemon juice

1 tbsp smooth Dijon mustard

1 tsp soy sauce

1/2 tsp liquid smoke

1/4 tsp ground white pepper

1/4 tsp celery salt

Potato Croutons

4 small waxy potatoes, such as fingerling, or new potatoes (unpeeled if organic)

3/4 tsp salt

1/2 tsp Italian seasoning blend

1/4 tsp freshly ground black pepper

1/8 tsp celery salt

6 tsp neutral-flavored oil

continued

↳ *Salad*

2 hearts Romaine lettuce, torn or sliced into strips

2 cups (500 mL) baby arugula

2 spring onions, thinly sliced on the bias

1 avocado, peeled, pitted, and diced

Other tasty additions to this salad include roasted asparagus, cubes of smoky, salty fried tofu or tempeh, diced tomatoes, or red bell peppers (raw or roasted).

Be sure to use waxy potatoes, as they will hold their shape best. After you've steamed them, rinse them to remove the starch that develops.

Minted Parsnip Coleslaw

Using red cabbage makes this raw slaw ever so pretty and pink. There's a wonderful contrast between the crunchy vegetables and creamy dressing that's enhanced by a hit of mint. Feel free to use green cabbage or a combination of red and green.

Make dressing

In a blender, pulse to combine all dressing ingredients. Add ¼ cup (60 mL) water and pulse until smooth. Add up to additional ¼ cup (60 mL) water and blend until thick and creamy, stopping to scrape down sides of blender jar as required.

Make coleslaw

Transfer dressing to a large bowl. Add shredded cabbage, parsnip, and carrot. Toss to coat with dressing. Stir in spring onions and mint. Taste and adjust seasoning as desired.

Serve immediately or chill until served.

Makes 6–8 servings

Dressing

1 medium ripe avocado

2 tbsp raw tahini

1/2 tsp lime zest

3 tbsp lime juice

1 garlic clove, chopped

1/2 tsp salt

pinch freshly ground black pepper

Coleslaw

3 cups (750 mL) shredded red cabbage

2 cups (500 mL) shredded parsnip

1 cup (250 mL) shredded carrot

1/4 cup (60 mL) finely chopped spring onions

1 1/2 tbsp finely chopped fresh mint

Radish & Carrot Citrus Slaw _gf_

This cabbage-based salad includes both the roots and tips of radishes and carrots and the complementary bright flavors of citrus. The natural flavors are enhanced, not coated, by the dressing. Serve immediately or chill before serving—it's great either way.

Makes 6 cups

1/4 cup (60 mL) Sweet Potato Mayo (p. 192) or your favorite vegan mayonnaise

2 tbsp orange juice

1 tbsp lime juice

1 tsp agave syrup

1/2 tsp lime zest

1/2 tsp orange zest

1/2 tsp lemon pepper seasoning

salt and freshly ground black pepper, to taste (optional)

6 cups (1.5 L) cored and shredded savoy cabbage

1/2 cup (125 mL) shredded radish greens

1 cup (250 mL) quartered and very thinly sliced radishes

1/2 cup (125 mL) quartered and very thinly sliced carrots

2 tbsp carrot greens, finely chopped

1 medium orange, peeled and segmented, pith removed

In a large bowl, whisk together mayonnaise, orange and lime juice, syrup, lime and orange zest, and lemon pepper seasoning. Taste and season with salt and pepper as desired.

Add cabbage, radish greens, radishes, carrots, and carrot greens. Toss to combine. Garnish with orange segments.

Watermelon radishes look especially pretty here.

Som Tum Salad   raw

If you've spent any time in Thailand, you know Som Tum—green papaya salad mixed with a mortar and pestle in street stalls all over the country. In my western kitchen-friendly version, a variety of root vegetables stands in for green papaya and a potato masher for the mortar and pestle.

In a large bowl, combine garlic, ginger, chile, lime juice, basil, spring onions, lemongrass, lime zest, syrup, and salt. Mash to make a loose paste, about 30 seconds.

Add grated sweet potatoes, daikon, and turnips. Using a potato masher, mash and toss to distribute aromatics evenly, about 1 minute. Add cherry tomatoes, green beans, carrots, chopped peanuts, and chopped cilantro. Mash and toss to just combine.

Garnish with whole peanuts, cilantro leaves, and lime wedges.

Best served right away, this salad will keep for up to a day.

This recipe is pretty spicy, like the original. If you're a bit of a heat wimp, use only 1 red chile or a milder chile such as jalapeño. You can always add more after tasting.

Makes 4–6 servings

2 garlic cloves, minced

1 tsp grated fresh ginger

2 small red chiles, minced (seeding optional)

2 tbsp lime juice

2 tbsp shredded basil leaves

1 tbsp finely sliced spring onions

1 tsp minced lemongrass, from 1 stalk

1/2 tsp lime zest

1/2 tsp agave syrup

1/4 tsp salt

1 cup (250 mL) peeled and grated white-fleshed sweet potatoes

1/2 cup (125 mL) peeled and grated daikon

1 cup (250 mL) peeled and grated turnips

1/2 cup (125 mL) cherry tomatoes, quartered

1/2 cup (125 mL) trimmed and thinly sliced green beans, cut on the bias to 1-in (2.5-cm) lengths

1/4 cup (60 mL) peeled carrot ribbons, using a potato peeler

1/4 cup (60 mL) raw peanuts, roughly chopped

1/4 cup (60 mL) finely chopped cilantro leaves

1/4 cup (60 mL) whole raw peanuts

1/4 cup (60 mL) cilantro leaves

1 lime, cut into 8 wedges

Pistachio & Cranberry Sweet Potato Salad

The dressing by itself is quite tangy but harmonizes perfectly with tender sweet potatoes and bursts of sweet cranberry.

Makes 4 servings

4 cups (1 L) peeled and cubed white-fleshed sweet potatoes

Dressing
1/2 cup (125 mL) soft or silken tofu
2 garlic cloves, chopped
3 tbsp flaxseed oil
3 tbsp white balsamic vinegar
1 1/2 tbsp nutritional yeast
1 tbsp lemon juice
1 tsp Dijon mustard
3/4 tsp salt
1/2 tsp agave syrup
1/4 tsp garlic powder
1/4 tsp freshly ground black pepper

1/4 cup (60 mL) pistachios
2 tbsp sliced dried cranberries

1 celery stalk, finely chopped
2 tbsp finely chopped spring onions

Steam sweet potatoes in a steamer basket over boiling water for 10–12 minutes, until tender when pierced with a knife.

While potatoes steam, make dressing. In a blender, combine all ingredients and purée until thick and smooth, stopping to scrape down sides of blender jar as required. Transfer to a large bowl and add pistachios and cranberries.

Remove sweet potatoes from steamer and combine with dressing.

Chill for at least an hour to allow dressing to be absorbed. Just before serving, stir in celery and spring onions. Taste and adjust seasoning as desired.

Adding the dressing to the sweet potatoes while they're still hot allows them to absorb the dressing as they cool. Because of this, the salad needs time to chill, so plan ahead.

Oca & Purple Potato Niçoise *gf*

Salty, briny olives, crisp green beans, creamy potatoes, and oca—this salad will whisk you off to the south of France with each bite. Serve at room temperature or chilled—delicious either way.

In a large mixing bowl, whisk together all dressing ingredients. Set aside.

Place potatoes and thyme sprig in a medium saucepan with enough water to just cover. Bring to a boil, reduce heat, and simmer for 5 minutes, until just tender. Using a slotted spoon, remove potatoes from water, place in a colander, and rinse under cold running water. Add to dressing in bowl and toss.

In same saucepan, bring water with thyme sprig to a boil, add green beans, and blanch by returning water to a boil and cooking for 1 minute from that point. Drain and rinse under cold running water to stop cooking process. Discard thyme. Add beans to potatoes in bowl and toss to combine.

Heat a grill pan or frying pan on medium-high. Lightly oil pan and grill oca pieces 5–8 minutes, turning frequently until tender and lined with grill marks on all sides. Remove from heat and add to potatoes and green beans in bowl. Toss to combine. Add tomatoes and olives and mix well. Taste and adjust seasoning as desired.

Line a large serving platter or individual plates with soft lettuce leaves and place tossed salad in middle of lettuce.

Canned olluco (see textbox, p. 108) needs only to be heated. Grill to give it marks.

Use small red-skinned or fingerling potatoes if you can't find purple ones.

Makes 2–4 servings

Dressing

3 tbsp olive oil

2 tbsp lemon juice

1 tbsp minced shallot

1 garlic clove, minced

1 tbsp minced capers

1 tbsp fresh tarragon, finely chopped

2 tsp Dijon mustard

1/4 tsp salt

1/8 tsp freshly ground black pepper

10 small purple potatoes, skin on, 8 oz (230 g), quartered lengthwise

1 sprig fresh thyme

8 oz (230 g) green beans, trimmed and cut into 2-in (5-cm) lengths

8 oz (230 g) oca, scrubbed and quartered lengthwise

1/2 cup (125 mL) seeded and roughly chopped Roma tomatoes

1/4 cup (60 mL) black olives, pitted and quartered

1/4 cup (60 mL) green olives, pitted and quartered

1 head soft lettuce, such as Bibb, Boston, or Butter, leaves roughly torn

⇢ *True Facts: Oca & Olluco*

Native to Peru and other Andean countries, these tubers can be used interchangeably in the recipes in this book.

Called oca or uqa, *Oxalis tuberosa* is known in New Zealand as the "New Zealand yam." The roots are small and brightly colored, often red, pink, yellow, or orange.

Latin American grocers may stock canned olluco, which you can use in place of fresh. Just skip the cooking step. Rinse canned vegetables thoroughly and heat through for a hot dish.

If you're having a hard time sourcing oca and olluco, you can use small waxy potatoes, fingerlings, or sunchokes, though cooking times may vary.

⇢ *Don't Throw Away the Skins*

The skins of any baked regular or sweet potatoes can be turned into an appetizer. Potato skins—hot, crispy, golden brown snacks—will fly off the plate. Serve with Rutabaga Pizza/ Pasta Sauce (p. 186), Avocado & Jicama Pico de Gallo (p. 196), or your favorite dips.

Cooking potatoes in advance is completely okay.

Use potato flesh as called for in a recipe and reserve skins.

In a deep fryer or large, deep pot, heat 2 in (5 cm) neutral-flavored oil to 375°F (190°C) on a deep-fry thermometer, or so that a small piece of potato dropped into hot oil immediately sizzles vigorously. Line a plate with paper towels to drain excess oil.

Allow oil to return to correct temperature between batches. Using metal tongs, and working in batches, carefully add skins to hot oil and fry for 2–3 minutes, until golden brown and crisp. Remove skins from oil with metal tongs and drain on paper towels. Season with salt and pepper, to taste.

Red Potato Salad

Red on so many levels, this spicy potato salad has creamy and crispy elements that will elevate any cookout, picnic, or barbecue—even a taco dinner. White-skinned potatoes can be used instead of red.

Preheat oven to 425°F (220°C).

In a small saucepan, cover Brazil nuts with water. Bring to a boil, reduce heat to medium, and simmer for 25–30 minutes, until easily pierced with a sharp knife.

In a small roasting pan, toss together potatoes, celery, olive oil, salt, and oregano.

In a second small roasting pan, combine bell peppers and tomatoes.

Place both pans in oven and roast for 20 minutes until potatoes are tender and golden in places, and peppers are charred and soft. Set pan with potatoes to one side.

Transfer peppers and tomatoes to a blender. Deglaze now-empty roasting pan with wine, then add wine and contents from pan to blender.

Drain Brazil nuts, and reserve cooking water. Add nuts to blender along with oil, chipotle and adobo sauce, syrup, salt, and black pepper. Add 6 tbsp reserved nut water to blender and carefully blend hot ingredients until smooth and creamy. The mixture should be medium consistency—not too thick, as potatoes will absorb some liquid as they chill. Transfer contents of blender to a large bowl.

Add contents of first roasting pan and mix to coat. Stir in remaining red bell peppers, celery, and spring onions.

Serve at room temperature or refrigerate for 1 hour and serve chilled.

Instead of cooking Brazil nuts, you can soak them for at least 24 hours before blending.

Makes 4 servings

1/2 cup (125 mL) raw Brazil nuts

1 1/2 lb (750 g) baby red-skinned potatoes, washed and halved
2 celery stalks, cut into 1-in (2.5-cm) lengths
1 tbsp olive oil
1/2 tsp salt
1/4 tsp dried oregano

1 red bell pepper, seeded and roughly chopped
1 large tomato, seeded and roughly chopped

2 tbsp red wine

1 tbsp flaxseed or olive oil
1 chipotle pepper in 1 tsp adobo sauce, seeded
1/2 tsp agave syrup
1/2 tsp salt
pinch freshly ground black pepper

1/2 red bell pepper, finely chopped
1 celery stalk, finely chopped
2 spring onions, finely chopped

Loaded Baked Potato Salad

Everyone's favorite. I've turned the familiar baked and loaded-with-sour-cream-bacon-bits-and-cheese potato into something completely different. Double the potato factor with the Crispy Potato Topping and enjoy.

Makes 4 servings

3 large Russet potatoes, about 12 oz (340 g) each

1 tsp olive oil

1/4 tsp salt

Bacon-y Bits

1 cup (250 mL) large unsweetened coconut shreds

2 tbsp + 1 tsp soy sauce

2 tsp liquid smoke

1/2 tsp smoked paprika

1/4 tsp ground fennel seeds

1/4 tsp celery salt

pinch each salt and freshly ground black pepper

Sour Cream-y Dressing

1/3 cup (80 mL) unsweetened soymilk

1 tbsp apple cider vinegar

1/2 cup (125 mL) soft tofu

5 tbsp grapeseed oil

2 tbsp lemon juice

2 tbsp white balsamic vinegar

1/2 tsp Dijon mustard

1/4 tsp salt

Preheat oven to 400°F (200°C).

Prick potatoes with a fork and rub with oil and salt. Bake potatoes for 1 hour, until tender. Make the toppings while potatoes bake or as they cool.

Make bits

In a medium bowl, toss coconut with soy sauce, liquid smoke, smoked paprika, ground fennel seeds, and celery salt. Spread seasoned coconut in a single layer on baking sheet.

Bake for 7–8 minutes, remove from oven, and stir. Return to oven for 5–6 more minutes more, stir again, and cook for 3–4 minutes. Ensure coconut browns but does not burn.

Remove from oven and sprinkle with a pinch of salt and pepper. Set aside to cool and crisp.

Make dressing

In a blender jar, mix soymilk and apple cider vinegar. Let sit for 2 minutes to curdle. Add remainder of ingredients and blend until smooth and creamy. Transfer to a large bowl and refrigerate.

Make sprinkles

In a spice grinder or food processor, combine hazelnuts, yeast, salt, pepper, thyme, and mustard, and grind to a medium-fine powder; a little texture but not big lumps of nuts.

Once potatoes are tender, remove from oven and let cool. Quarter lengthwise and remove flesh, leaving a thin strip of skin.

Cut flesh into 1-in (2.5-cm) pieces and add to Sour Cream-y dressing, along with chopped chives or spring onions. Refrigerate until ready to serve.

Make topping

Cut potato skins widthwise into thin ¼-in (6-mm) strips.

In a large frying pan on high, heat oil until a small piece of potato dropped into hot oil immediately sizzles vigorously.

Add potato strips and fry for 7–10 minutes, tossing often with tongs, until crispy and golden brown.

Drain on paper towels and let cool slightly.

Make salad

Top potatoes in dressing with Bacon-y Bits, Cheese-y Sprinkles, and Crispy Potato Topping or serve on the side and let each guest add their own.

This recipe has many steps but comes with built-in cheats. If you're short on time, use commercial replacements for vegan bacon bits, vegan Parmesan, and sour cream dressing (and adjust flavors to taste).

The potatoes can be baked (or barbecued) in advance and added to the salad a day later.

Leftover Bacon-y Bits and Cheese-y Sprinkles will keep in a sealed container in the refrigerator for up to a week.

Cheese-y Sprinkles
1/4 cup (60 mL) toasted hazelnuts, skins rubbed off as much as possible
1 1/2 tbsp nutritional yeast
1/2 tsp salt
1/8 tsp freshly ground black pepper
1/8 tsp dried thyme
1/8 tsp dried mustard

1/4 cup (60 mL) finely chopped chives or spring onions

Crispy Potato Topping (optional)
1/4 cup (60 mL) neutral-flavored oil
potato skins

Rutabaga & Pumpkin Salad with Toasted Pumpkin Seeds gf

This salad is perfect for those cooler evenings when summer has waned and autumn has arrived. It offers the comfort of a fall dish and the presentation and intensity of a summer one.

Makes 3 cups (750 mL)

1/2 cup (125 mL) pumpkin seeds

1/2 medium rutabagas, cubed
1/2 medium pumpkin or winter squash, cubed

2 tbsp olive oil
2 tbsp apricot jam
2 tbsp lemon juice
1/2 tsp dried sage
1/4 tsp salt
1/8 tsp freshly ground black pepper

2 tbsp dried apricots, thinly sliced
2 cups (500 mL) arugula or other bitter greens

In a large frying pan on medium, heat pumpkin seeds for 3–4 minutes, until toasted and starting to pop. Remove from pan, spread on a large plate, and let cool.

Fit large saucepan with a steamer basket. Add water to reach bottom of basket. Bring to a boil, and add rutabaga and pumpkin. Steam for 8–10 minutes, until tender.

Meanwhile, using a spice grinder or food processor, grind half the pumpkin seeds. Transfer to a large bowl.

Whisk ground pumpkin seeds with oil, jam, lemon juice, sage, salt, and pepper to make a dressing.

Toss warm vegetables in dressing. Chill for 30 minutes in refrigerator.

Toss with remaining whole pumpkin seeds, sliced apricots, and arugula just before serving.

Kohlrabi, Lentil & Barley Salad

*Drawing on kohlrabi's Eastern European roots, this fusion-inspired salad could be
your inspiration to add more kohlrabi to your diet. Serve at room temperature or chilled.*

Makes 4–6 servings

2 medium kohlrabi, peeled and diced
2 tsp olive oil
1/2 tsp salt
1/4 tsp paprika
1/8 tsp freshly ground black pepper
1/16 tsp ground fennel seeds
1/16 tsp ground sumac

3/4 cup (175 mL) green lentils, rinsed
1/2 cup (125 mL) pearl barley, rinsed

2 tbsp olive oil
2 tsp apple cider vinegar
2 tsp red wine vinegar
1 tsp Dijon mustard
1/4 tsp salt
1/8 tsp paprika
1/8 tsp freshly ground black pepper
1/8 tsp ground fennel seeds
1/8 tsp ground sumac

1/4 cup (60 mL) finely chopped celery
1/4 cup (60 mL) flat-leaf parsley, finely
  chopped
1 tbsp finely chopped red onions
1 tbsp finely chopped fresh tarragon
1/2 tsp finely chopped fresh thyme

Preheat oven to 425°F (220°C). Line a baking sheet with parchment paper.

In a large bowl, toss together kohlrabi, 2 tsp oil, salt, paprika, pepper, fennel seed, and sumac. Spread in a single layer on prepared sheet and roast for 30 minutes, until kohlrabi is very soft and lightly browned. Toss halfway through roasting time.

Meanwhile, bring a medium saucepan of water to a boil. Add lentils and barley. Reduce heat to medium-low and simmer, uncovered, for 22–25 minutes until tender but firm. Drain and rinse under cold running water.

In a large bowl, whisk together 2 tbsp oil, vinegars, mustard, salt, paprika, pepper, fennel seed, and sumac. Stir in celery, parsley, onions, tarragon, and thyme. Stir in cooled barley and lentils.

Add roasted kohlrabi, and stir to combine. Taste and adjust seasoning as desired.

Marinated Turnip Caprese Salad

Okay, so you'll never mistake the crisp crunch of raw turnip for mozzarella, but the flavors and look of a traditional Caprese are captured in this inspired raw re-invention.

Makes 2–4 servings

2 1/2 tbsp lemon juice

2 tbsp white balsamic or apple cider vinegar

2 tbsp water

2 tbsp olive oil

1/2 tsp dried basil

1/2 tsp salt

1/4 tsp dried oregano

1/4 tsp freshly ground black pepper

1 bay leaf

1 small turnip, peeled

3 large vine-ripened tomatoes, sliced 1/4-in (6 mm) thick

1 bunch fresh basil

pinch sea salt
freshly cracked black pepper

In a large resealable plastic bag, combine lemon juice, vinegar, water, olive oil, basil, salt, oregano, ¼ tsp pepper, and bay leaf.

Using a mandoline, slicer blade in a food processor, or very sharp knife, slice turnip into ¼-in (6-mm) rounds. Poke each slice all over with a fork. Add turnip rounds to marinade, coat well, and let marinate for at least 1 hour.

Remove turnip slices from marinade, discarding bay leaf. Arrange turnip slices on a platter, alternating with tomato slices and basil leaves in an overlapping circle; turnip, tomato, basil, repeat, tucking the last tomato slice and basil leaf under the first turnip slice laid.

Sprinkle with a pinch of salt and black pepper, and serve with remaining marinade on the side.

Celeriac Celery Waldorf Salad

Like a traditional Waldorf, this salad pops with celery, apple, and walnuts, but also showcases the mellow sweetness of raw celeriac in a way you'll find familiar.

In a large bowl, whisk together mayonnaise, celery leaves, lemon juice and zest, salt, dill, and celery seeds.

Add celeriac and apples. Stir to combine. Stir in red grapes, walnuts, and celery. Garnish with celery leaves and walnuts.

This salad is a good make-ahead because you can also serve it chilled.

Makes 4–6 servings

1/3 cup (80 mL) Sweet Potato Mayo (p. 192) or favorite vegan mayonnaise

2 tbsp finely chopped celery leaves

1 tbsp lemon juice

1 tsp lemon zest

1/4 tsp salt

1/8 tsp dried dill

1/8 tsp celery seeds

1 cup (250 mL) celeriac, trimmed, peeled, and coarsely grated

1 sweet apple, such as Gala, cored and diced

1/2 cup (125 mL) red grapes, quartered

1/2 cup (125 mL) walnut pieces

2 celery stalks, diced

2 tbsp celery leaves

2 tbsp walnut halves

Parsnip Tabouleh

Bursting with fresh herb flavors and brightened by lemon, this gluten-free and grain-free version of the Middle Eastern staple uses parsnips instead of traditional bulgur wheat.

Makes 2–4 servings

1 tbsp olive oil

3/4 cup (175 mL) finely chopped parsnips

1 garlic clove, minced

1 shallot, minced

1 celery stalk, finely chopped

3/4 cup (175 mL) peeled and finely grated
  parsnips

3 tbsp lemon juice

1 tsp lemon zest

3/4 cup (175 mL) flat-leaf parsley, minced

1/2 cup (125 mL) curly leaf parsley, minced

1/2 cup (125 mL) mint, minced

1/2 cup (125 mL) seeded and finely chopped
  Roma tomatoes

2 spring onions, finely chopped

1/2 tsp salt

1/8 tsp freshly ground black pepper

In a large frying pan on medium, heat oil. Add chopped parsnips, garlic, shallots, and celery. Sauté for 7–8 minutes, until soft and golden brown. Remove from heat and let cool in pan as you prepare the rest of the salad.

In a large bowl, mix together grated parsnips, lemon juice, and lemon zest. Add parsley, mint, tomatoes, spring onions, salt, pepper, and cooked vegetables to bowl and mix to combine well.

Chill for 1 hour before serving.

Sunchoke & Artichoke Heart Quinoa Salad

Start to cook the quinoa before you make the dressing so it's ready to add with the cooked sunchokes. Served warm, sunchokes are soft and tender; when chilled, they're crisp. Either way, they're good—I like to serve them warm one day and chilled for lunch the next. (See photo, p. 113)

In a blender, combine 2 artichoke hearts with their brine, oil, yeast, hemp seeds, and parsley. Blend until smooth. Taste and adjust seasoning with salt and pepper as desired. Transfer to a large bowl.

Bring a medium saucepan of salted water to a boil. Cut sunchokes into wedges the length of the root and ¼-in (6-mm) at their widest. Cook sunchokes in water for 6 minutes, until tender and thin edges are translucent. Drain.

Add to dressing while still warm. Toss to coat. Stir in quinoa, sliced artichoke hearts, green peas, and spring onions.

To make cooked quinoa for this salad, start with ½ cup (125 mL) dry quinoa, rinsed.

Makes 4–6 servings

2 artichoke hearts (canned)
6 tbsp liquid (brine) from artichokes
6 tbsp olive oil
2 tbsp nutritional yeast
2 tbsp hemp seeds
2 tbsp roughly chopped parsley
salt and freshly ground black pepper, to taste

3 medium to large sunchokes, scrubbed

1 1/2 cups (375 mL) cooked quinoa
4 artichoke hearts (canned), sliced lengthwise into 6 wedges
1/2 cup (125 mL) frozen peas, thawed in boiling water
2 spring onions, thinly sliced on the bias

Burdock & Bok Choi Udon Noodle Salad

Serve this loosely Japanese-inspired salad as a stand-alone lunch or as a vibrant side dish, either chilled or at room temperature.

Makes 2–4 servings

2 4-oz (115- g) bunches udon noodles

6 oz (175 g) burdock, about 14 in (35 cm) long
1 tbsp lemon juice

Dressing
2 tbsp orange juice
1 tbsp lemon juice
1 tbsp lime juice
1 tbsp agave syrup
1 tbsp soy sauce
1 tbsp sesame oil
3 tbsp flaxseed oil

2 tsp sesame oil
2 garlic cloves

1/4 tsp salt
12 oz (340 g) baby bok choy, leaves shredded into 1/8-in (3-mm) widths and stems cut into 1/4-in (6-mm) lengths

1 tsp black sesame seeds
1 tsp white sesame seeds

2 spring onions, thinly sliced
1 orange, peeled and segmented

In a medium saucepan bring salted water to a boil. Add udon noodles and cook 10 minutes, until very tender.

While noodles cook, prepare burdock and dressing. In a medium bowl combine 1 tbsp lemon juice with 2 cups (500 mL) water. Peel burdock, and using a vegetable peeler, shave burdock into long thin strips. Place shavings immediately in lemon water to prevent discoloration.

In a large bowl, whisk together all dressing ingredients.

Drain and rinse cooked noodles under cold running water. Toss in dressing and set aside.

In a large frying pan on medium-high, heat 2 tsp sesame oil. Sauté garlic for 30 seconds until fragrant.

Drain burdock and sauté for 2 minutes with salt. Add bok choy stems and sauté for 3 minutes, until lightly browned and softened but still firm. Add burdok and bok choy to noodles. Toss. Add shredded bok choy leaves, sesame seeds, and toss to combine well.

Garnish with spring onions and orange segments.

Mango & Mint Riced Salad Lettuce Cups

Serve these pretty lettuce cups as a finger food appetizer or on a buffet table for a healthy touch of something fancy. The filling on its own makes a wonderful salad full of bright flavors and tempting colors.

In a small bowl, cover cashews with 1 cup (250 mL) warm water and soak for 15 minutes until softened. Drain and discard soaking water. Transfer to food processor, along with jicama, 2 tbsp lime juice, oil, salt, and pepper. Pulse until nuts and jicama are the size of rice grains, but not smooth.

Transfer to a large bowl. Stir in mango, avocado, red bell peppers, mint, and cilantro. Taste and adjust seasoning, adding remaining tbsp of lime juice as desired.

Place 2 tbsp of filling into the "bowl" of each lettuce leaf and garnish with a mint leaf.

You can substitute peeled and grated parsnips (2 medium) for the chopped jicama. Though not as moist, the result is just as tasty.

Makes 24 lettuce cups

1/2 cup (125 mL) raw cashews

1 small jicama, peeled and roughly
  chopped
2 tbsp lime juice, plus 1 tbsp for seasoning
1 1/2 tbsp flaxseed oil
1/2 tsp salt
1/8 tsp freshly ground black pepper

3/4 cup (175 mL) peeled, seeded, and cubed
  mango
1/2 cup (125 mL) peeled, seeded, and cubed
  avocado
1/2 red bell pepper, finely chopped
1/4 packed cup (60 mL) finely chopped
  fresh mint
1/4 cup (60 mL) cilantro, finely chopped

24 soft lettuce leaves from 2 heads, such as
  Boston or Bibb

24 mint leaves to garnish

Fresh Jicama Nacho Salad with Raw Beet Chili *gf* *raw*

Satisfying and filling, this is the perfect chili for the middle of summer.

Makes 4–6 servings

1/2 cup (125 mL) walnut pieces

3 tbsp lime juice
1/2 cup (125 mL) warm water
pinch salt

1 medium jicama

1/2 cup (125 mL) finely grated red beet
1/2 red bell pepper, seeded and roughly chopped
1 jalapeño, roughly chopped (seeding optional)
2 Roma tomatoes, seeded and roughly chopped
1 garlic clove, finely chopped
1/4 cup (60 mL) cilantro leaves
1/4 tsp cumin
1/4 tsp paprika
1/2 tsp salt
1/8 tsp freshly ground black pepper
1/8 tsp ground fennel seeds

1 cup (250 mL) shredded lettuce
1/2 cup (125 mL) grated carrot
1 avocado, cubed
4–6 cilantro sprigs, for garnish

In a small bowl, soak walnut pieces in ½ cup (125 mL) water for at least 20 minutes while preparing other ingredients.

In a large resealable plastic bag, combine lime juice, water, and salt.

Peel jicama and quarter. Using a mandoline or very sharp knife, thinly slice into ⅛ in (3 mm) rounds. Place rounds in resealable plastic bag and marinate in lime juice mixture for at least 10 minutes while preparing remaining ingredients.

Transfer drained soaked walnuts to food processor. Add beets, bell peppers, jalapeño, tomatoes, garlic, cilantro, cumin, paprika, salt, black pepper, and fennel. Pulse until well combined but not smooth, stopping to scrape down sides of bowl as required. Makes about 1 ½ cups (375 mL) chili. Taste and adjust seasoning as desired.

Arrange jicama "nacho" slices on a large serving platter or individual plates. Top with lettuce, beet chili, carrots, avocado, and cilantro.

Truly Traditional Sides

When most people think of root vegetables, they probably imagine side dishes. Throughout this book, I've included some traditional options, such as chipped (pp. 53, 91, 141), mashed (pp. 126, 129, 136) and roasted (pp. 32, 52, 78, 132, 134, 138). In this chapter, I've tried to expand the scope of what root vegetables can do. Open your mind and tickle your taste buds.

↪ *Tips for Perfect Mashed Potatoes*

Choose the potato variety with care. For a fluffy mash, don't use waxy potatoes. Yellow or white is fine, but a high-starch potato, such as Russet, works best (see p. 29). Allow 1 medium potato per person (peeling optional).

- Fill a saucepan with cold water. As you cut potatoes, place them immediately into water so they don't discolor. Lightly salt the water.

- Bring to a boil on high heat, then reduce to medium-low and simmer until tender and starting to fall apart, about 20 minutes. Potatoes should almost collapse when a knife is inserted.

- Drain potatoes in a colander, leaving less than ¼ cup (60 mL) cooking water still clinging to potatoes, then return to saucepan.

- Add enough milk to saucepan to reach half the height of the potatoes and 2–3 tbsp vegan margarine. (To make a lower-fat mash, use potato cooking water instead of milk and margarine.)

- Return to stovetop. On medium-low, melt margarine and heat milk before mashing. When milk is nearly boiling, remove from heat and add 1–2 tsp Dijon mustard, to taste. This adds a burst of umami which is very pleasant.

- Using some elbow grease, mash to remove lumps. For completely smooth mashed potatoes, pass through a food mill or press through a wide-meshed sieve. Taste and season—be generous with the salt and pepper.

- On occasion, I like to change it up by adding one of the following: roasted garlic, chives, spring onions, roasted red bell peppers, barbecued corn kernels, or vegan sour cream or cream cheese, mashing to combine.

Potato & Kohlrabi Rosti

Rosti is a combination of crisp, golden brown crust concealing tender, melt-in-your-mouth roots. Don't limit the accent vegetable to kohlrabi. Any root veggie that can be eaten raw (parsnips, carrots, or sunchokes, for example) can be substituted, giving the dish a subtly different flavor.

Fill medium saucepan with water and bring to a boil.

Using a box grater or food processor, coarsely grate potato. Blanch potato shreds by adding to boiling water and returning water to a boil. Drain and immediately rinse under cold water until cool to touch. Drain again.

Squeeze out excess water from blanched potatoes with your hands (they will be a little slimy), and transfer to a large mixing bowl. Add kohlrabi, starch, salt, dill, thyme, and pepper. Mix well.

In a medium frying pan on medium to medium-high, heat oil. Have ready a second frying pan or plate that fits inside first frying pan. When oil is hot, add potato-kohlrabi mixture to pan and spread to edges. Place second frying pan (or plate) on top to flatten vegetables as rosti cooks. You may need to place something heavy, such as a glass mixing bowl, on top of the pan or plate. Fry for 10–12 minutes, until bottom and sides are golden brown and crisp.

Invert onto plate, slice into wedges, and serve.

This recipe blanches potatoes before frying for two reasons: first, when done in advance it cuts down on the time needed for frying; second, it ensures the potatoes are completely cooked.

Makes 2 servings

8 oz (230 g) red-skinned potatoes (peeling optional)

6 oz (175 g) kohlrabi, peeled and grated
4 tsp potato starch
1/2 tsp salt
1/4 tsp dried dill
1/4 tsp dried thyme
pinch freshly ground black pepper

2 tbsp neutral-flavored oil

Kalecannon & Avocado gf

This is my take on the traditional Irish colcannon. Adding avocado may seem strange, but it's really yummy and gives a creamy richness to the dish. (If you're not a fan, simply leave it out.)

In a large frying pan on medium, heat oil and sauté onions and garlic for 5 minutes until lightly browned. Add kale, cover, and steam for 3–5 minutes, until bright green and tender.

Add potatoes and stir to combine. Cook for 5 minutes, until just lightly browned, stirring so potatoes don't stick or burn. Remove from heat and stir in avocado. Taste and adjust seasoning as desired.

Next time you have mashed potatoes for dinner, cook extra so you'll be ready to make this dish the next day.

Makes 2 servings

1 tsp neutral-flavored oil

1/4 cup (60 mL) sliced onions
2 garlic cloves, minced

1 1/2 cups (375 mL) shredded kale
1 cup (250 mL) leftover mashed potatoes, at
   room temperature

1/2 ripe avocado, chopped

salt and freshly ground black pepper, to
   taste

Potato Croquettes gf

Filling and warming, these lightly spiced croquettes make an ideal side dish for an Indian fusion meal, a light lunch topped with sautéed spinach or served with a salad of leafy greens. Once formed, croquettes can be kept in the refrigerator for up to 2 days, until ready to cook. (See photo, p. 170)

Makes 4–6 servings

2/3 cup (160 mL) chickpea flour
1/2 tsp salt
1/2 tsp cumin seeds
1/4 tsp onion powder
1/4 tsp garlic powder
1/4 tsp curry powder, more to taste

2 cups (500 mL) cold mashed potatoes
1/4 cup (60 mL) parsley or cilantro, finely chopped

1 tbsp coconut oil

In a large dry frying pan on medium heat, combine chickpea flour, salt, cumin seeds, onion powder, garlic powder, and curry powder for 7–8 minutes, stirring frequently, until golden and fragrant. Remove from heat and transfer to a large bowl. Set frying pan aside.

Add mashed potatoes and parsley to flour mixture. Mix until well distributed and mixture is stiff.

Divide dough into 16 even pieces, shaping into 2-in (5-cm) discs. Using your thumb, lightly indent center of discs.

In same frying pan on medium-high, heat oil. Add croquettes, frying in batches to avoid overcrowding pan, for 3–4 minutes, until golden and crisp. Flip carefully and cook for 3–4 minutes, until second side is also golden.

Frybake Potatoes gf option

My mother made a dish similar to this when we were growing up.
At the time, we didn't appreciate how good it was.

Preheat oven to 400°F (200°C).

In a wide shallow bowl, combine yeast, panko, herbs, and salt and pepper.

Pour oil into a 9 x 13 in (3.5 L), or larger, casserole dish and heat in oven for 5 minutes.

Halve potatoes lengthwise. Remove dish from oven. Dip cut surface of potato into seasoning mix, then carefully place cut-side down in hot oil.

Carefully cover hot dish with aluminum foil and bake for 35–40 minutes, until potatoes are easily pierced with a fork. Increase oven temperature to 425°F (220°C), uncover potatoes, and cook for 15–20 minutes, until cut sides are browned and crispy.

The recipe is not missing a step. My testers wanted to make sure I pointed out clearly that the potatoes do not get turned at all.

You can change the herbs to suit the food you're serving with the potatoes. I've used combinations of cumin, paprika, and oregano, as well as tarragon, marjoram, and oregano.

Makes 4 servings

1 1/2 tbsp nutritional yeast
1 1/2 tbsp panko or gluten-free breadcrumbs
1 1/2 tsp dried, crumbled sage
1 1/2 tsp dried thyme
1 1/2 tsp dried rosemary
1 tsp salt, or to taste
freshly ground black pepper, to taste

3 tbsp neutral-flavored oil
3 lb (1.5 kg) white or Yukon Gold potatoes, scrubbed, peel on

Roasted Reds & Whites & Greens

Another "root to tip" recipe using slightly bitter greens and roots sweet from roasting.
So pretty on the plate, so tasty in your mouth.

Makes 4 servings

1 1/2 tbsp olive oil

4 garlic cloves, peeled

1/2 tsp salt

1/2 tsp smoked paprika

1/2 tsp ground cumin

1/4 tsp ancho chile powder

1/4 tsp dried oregano

1/8 tsp cayenne, to taste (optional)

8 oz (230 g) radishes, trimmed and quartered, greens removed, and 1 cup (250 mL) greens reserved

1 1/2 lb (750 g) beets, trimmed and diced, greens removed and 2 cups (500 mL) smallest, most tender leaves reserved

Preheat oven to 450°F (230°C). Line a baking sheet with parchment paper.

In a large bowl, combine oil, garlic, salt, paprika, cumin, chile powder, oregano, and cayenne. Add radishes and beets and toss to fully coat. Transfer to baking sheet and spread in a single layer. Set aside bowl but don't rinse.

Roast for 10 minutes, toss, and roast for 10 more minutes, until vegetables are completely tender. While roots roast, shred radish and beet greens. Place in previously used bowl.

Remove cooked roots from oven and transfer to bowl along with any seasonings on baking sheet. Toss roots and greens together for 2 minutes to lightly wilt greens.

Red beets will color the radishes an intense red. If you can find them, try chioggia beets. They're the pretty white and red ones — the same colors as radishes.

If the beets or radishes don't come with greens attached, you can still make this recipe — just skip the last step where you prepare the greens, or add shredded arugula or Swiss chard instead.

Stovetop-Roasted Parsnips & Brussels Sprouts

Parsnips are underrated. They also do themselves no favors because, when they grow big, they become unpleasantly woody. But catch them small and cook them properly, and they're sweet, creamy, and very more-ish. I've combined them here with another vegetable that I adore, the humble Brussels sprout. They're cooked on low heat to tenderize, then blasted with high heat to caramelize. Yum!

Makes 4 servings

1 tbsp olive oil
2 garlic cloves, minced
1 shallot, minced
1 tbsp minced fresh ginger

1/2 tsp Chinese 5-spice powder
1 tbsp soy sauce

1/2 lb (250 g) parsnips, peeled and cut into strips 2 in (5 cm) long and 1/4 in (6 mm) wide
1/2 lb (250 g) Brussels sprouts, trimmed, large ones quartered and small ones halved

In a large frying pan on low, heat oil. Sauté garlic, shallots, and ginger for 2–3 minutes, until fragrant. Add 5-spice powder and soy sauce, mix well, and sauté for 1 minute.

Add parsnips and sprouts, toss to coat in spices, cover, and cook, stirring occasionally, until just tender when pierced with a knife, about 8 minutes. Uncover and increase heat to medium-high. Cook, stirring occasionally, until partly golden brown and tender, 3–4 minutes. Serve hot.

To save preparation time, prepare Brussels sprouts up to a day in advance and store in a bag in refrigerator until ready to use. If you want to prepare parsnips in advance, store covered with water, or they will oxidize and brown.

Sweet & Heat Glazed Sweet Potatoes

There's a surprise hiding in this soft, sweet, and sticky side dish—a wee kick of spice.

Preheat oven to 425°F (220°C). Line a large baking sheet with parchment paper.

In a large bowl, combine oil with sweet potatoes, salt, and pepper. Toss to coat. Spread coated sweet potatoes in a single layer on baking sheet. Bake for 15 minutes, until tender and a little browned.

While potatoes bake, prepare glazes.

Make sweet glaze

In a medium bowl, mix all ingredients until well combined.

Make hot glaze

In a small bowl, mix all ingredients until well combined.

Once potatoes are tender and browned, remove from oven.

Transfer two-thirds of potatoes to bowl containing sweet glaze and toss to coat. Transfer remaining third of potatoes to bowl containing heat glaze and toss to coat.

Return potatoes to baking sheet, putting sweet-glazed at one end and heat-glazed potatoes at other end. Don't mix flavors just yet.

Bake for 10 minutes, until soft, sticky, and perfectly tender. Remove from oven, transfer to large serving bowl, and toss to combine.

Makes 4 servings

2 tbsp neutral-flavored oil

1 1/2 lb (750 g) white-fleshed sweet potatoes, peeled and cubed

3/4–1 lb (340–500 g) orange-fleshed sweet potatoes, peeled and cubed

1 tsp salt

1/8 tsp freshly ground black pepper

Sweet Glaze

2 tbsp brown rice syrup

2 tbsp agave syrup

1/4 tsp ground cinnamon

pinch ground nutmeg

Heat Glaze

2 tbsp maple syrup

1 1/2 tsp Sriracha or other hot sauce

1/2 tsp smoked paprika

1/2 tsp garlic powder

Turnip & Cauliflower Mash gf

If you need a break from standard mashed potatoes but still want something earthy and comforting, look no further.

Makes 2 to 4 servings

2 medium turnips, peeled and cubed

1/2 head cauliflower, trimmed, stalks and
  florets cut into 1/2-in (1-cm) pieces

pinch salt

2 tbsp vegan margarine (optional)

1 tsp Dijon mustard

1/2 tsp salt

1/8 tsp freshly ground black pepper

2 tbsp finely chopped fresh chives

In a large saucepan, combine turnips, cauliflower, and salt. Cover with water, and bring to a boil on high. Reduce heat to medium-high and cook, uncovered, for 12–15 minutes, until perfectly tender.

Drain, reserving ¼ cup (60 mL) cooking liquid. Transfer vegetables to food processor. Add margarine, mustard, salt, and pepper. Pulse until smooth and creamy. Add cooking liquid by the tablespoonful until it reaches desired consistency. Stir in chives. Taste and adjust seasoning as desired.

Turn leftovers into croquettes using the method for Potato Croquettes (p. 130); just increase chickpea flour by 2 tbsp. These croquettes won't be as firm as those made with potatoes.

Sweetly Spiced Carrots gf

Bold flavors of garlic, ginger, and jalapeño enhanced by agave syrup bring out carrots' natural sweetness. This dish is easy to prepare and makes a tasty side with any meal. (See photo, p. 170)

In a large frying pan on medium-high, heat oil. Add cumin seeds, allow to sizzle, and immediately toss with carrots. Cover and cook for 5 minutes, stirring occasionally, until tender and partly browned.

Add garlic, ginger, and jalapeños. Cook uncovered, stirring constantly, until fragrant, for 30 seconds. Remove from heat, add syrup, and stir to coat. Taste and adjust seasoning as desired.

Makes 2–4 servings

1 tbsp olive oil
1/2 tsp cumin seeds

2 cups (500 mL) peeled and sliced carrots,
    rounds less than 1/8 in (3 mm) thick

1 garlic clove, minced
1 tbsp ginger, minced
1/2 jalapeño, minced

1 tsp agave syrup

salt and pepper to taste

Roasted Kohlrabi & Broccoli *gf*

Kohlrabi and broccoli are cousins, botanically speaking, and they're a perfect pairing in this simple, very tasty side dish.

Makes 2–4 servings

1 head broccoli, stem peeled and cubed, florets cut into 1/2-in (1-cm) pieces

3 medium kohlrabi, peeled and cut into 1/2-in (1-cm) pieces

1 jalapeño, seeded and minced

2 garlic cloves, minced

2 tbsp olive oil

1 tsp salt

1/8 tsp freshly ground black pepper

Preheat oven to 425°F (220°C). Line a large baking sheet with parchment paper.

In a large bowl, toss together all ingredients. Rub oil and seasonings into the vegetables. Spread in a single layer on prepared sheet.

Roast for 15 minutes, remove from oven, toss vegetables, and return to oven. Roast for another 10–15 minutes, until florets are browned and crisp, and broccoli stems and kohlrabi are perfectly tender and partly browned.

This recipe doesn't call for kohlrabi greens. If you have some, use the perfectly tasty leaves in Kohlrabi Greens Garnish (p. 159) to serve alongside this dish or on mashed potatoes.

Baked Oca with Simple No-Cook Peanut or BBQ Sauce (gf) (cn) (peanut option)

This South American root suits both the creamy, mild Ecuadorean-inspired peanut sauce and the more vibrant easy-to-make barbecue sauce. I couldn't decide which I preferred, so I've included both.

Preheat oven to 400°F (200°C). Line a baking sheet with parchment paper.

Place oca on sheet and bake for 18–22 minutes, until tender. While oca bakes, make sauce of choice.

Make peanut sauce

Over a medium bowl using a microplane or the fine side of a box grater, grate tomato and bell pepper. Do not use grated skins; just discard them.

Grate garlic into tomatoes and peppers. Add peanut butter, 1 tbsp water, salt, and pepper. Whisk until smooth and well combined. Add additional water by the teaspoon to reach desired consistency. Taste and adjust seasoning. Set aside.

Make BBQ sauce

In a small bowl, whisk 1 tbsp water with all ingredients until well combined.

Once oca is tender, remove from oven and let sit until cool enough to handle. Halve oca lengthwise. Ladle sauce over slices, or serve on the side.

For information on using oca, see p. 108.

If using canned olluco or oca, drain, rinse, and halve vegetable lengthwise. In a large frying pan on medium-high, heat 2 tsp neutral-flavored oil and sauté for 2 minutes per side until heated through and lightly browned before serving with sauce.

Makes 2 servings

10 oz (300 g) oca (10–12), scrubbed and pricked with fork

No-Cook Peanut Sauce
2 medium tomatoes, seeded and quartered
1/2 medium red bell pepper, seeded and quartered

1 garlic clove
1/4 cup (60 mL) smooth natural peanut butter
1/4 tsp salt
1/8 tsp freshly ground black pepper

No-Cook BBQ Sauce
1 tbsp neutral-flavored oil
1 tbsp tomato paste
1 tbsp soy sauce
1 tbsp pomegranate molasses
1 tbsp maple syrup
1 tsp liquid smoke
1/2 tsp Dijon mustard
1/2 tsp garlic powder

Celeriac-Infused Bubble & Squeak *gf*

Rustic and homey (which, in cookbook terms, translates as ugly), these patties are pure comfort food. I have elevated the humble Bubble & Squeak (traditionally a way to use up leftovers) with the addition of celeriac, caraway, and peas.

Makes 2–4 servings

1 small celeriac, scrubbed

2 large white or Yukon Gold potatoes, scrubbed

6 tbsp unsweetened nondairy milk

1 tsp Dijon mustard

1/2 tsp salt

1/8 tsp freshly ground black pepper

1 tbsp coconut oil

1/2 medium onion, thinly sliced

1/4 tsp ground caraway seeds

5 cups (1.25 L) shredded Savoy cabbage

2 tbsp stock or water

1/2 cup (125 mL) thawed frozen peas (optional)

1/2 tbsp coconut oil, plus additional oil as needed

Preheat oven to 400°F (200°C).

Pierce celeriac and potatoes with a fork. Bake for 75–85 minutes, until they are very tender and can be pierced with a knife. Remove from oven and set aside for 20 minutes, until cool enough to handle.

Halve potatoes, scoop out 1 ½ cups (375 mL) flesh, and place in large bowl. Roughly mash to break up lumps.

Halve celeriac, scoop or cut out ¾ cup (175 mL) flesh, and transfer to food processor along with milk, mustard, salt, and pepper. Blend until thick and smooth. Add to bowl with potatoes.

In a large frying pan on medium-high, heat 1 tbsp oil. Add onions and sauté for 2 minutes, until soft and lightly browned. Add caraway seeds and sauté for 30 seconds. Add cabbage and stock. Cover and cook, stirring occasionally for 3 minutes, until softened and just starting to partly brown. Transfer to bowl with mashed potato mixture. Add peas and mix to combine well. Taste and adjust seasoning as desired.

Reheat frying pan on medium and melt ½ tbsp oil.

Form ½ cup (125 mL) mounds of mixture in pan. Gently press mounds to form roughly 3-in (8-cm) circles. Do not over-crowd pan. Cook for 2 minutes per side, until they form golden brown crusts and are heated through.

While this recipe looks involved, you can complete a number of steps in advance. Roast the vegetables when the oven is already on for something else. Assembled and uncooked, Bubble & Squeak can be kept in the refrigerator for up to 3 days.

Another cheat is to skip the roasted potatoes, using instead the same amount of any leftover mashed potatoes. You can also substitute the same amount of any cooked root vegetable for the cooked celeriac.

Reserve the skins of the potatoes to make Potato Skins (p. 108).

Seasoned Yuca Fries gf

What would you call the transformation of a bland, boring, starchy root into a light, airy, crispy bite of deliciousness? I call it this recipe, and it's pure magic.

Fill a medium saucepan with water and bring to a boil on high. Add yuca strips and return water to a boil. Reduce to medium-high, and cook 12–15 minutes, until yuca is very tender when pierced and edges are translucent. Drain yuca, rinse under cold running water, and spread on a clean tea towel to absorb excess water. Pat dry.

In a deep fryer or large pot on high, heat 3 in (8 cm) neutral-flavored oil to 375°F (190°C) on a deep-fry thermometer, or so that a small piece of yuca dropped into hot oil immediately sizzles vigorously.

While oil heats and yuca dries, make seasoning sprinkle and dipping sauce:

In a large bowl, combine salt, lime zest, cumin, and pepper.

In a small bowl, whisk together sauce, juices, jam, syrup, and hot sauce. Taste and adjust seasoning as desired.

Line a large plate with paper towels.

When oil is hot, fry yuca, working in batches to avoid overcrowding pot, for 3–4 minutes, until lightly golden, crispy, and crunchy-looking.

Transfer cooked yuca to paper towels to absorb excess oil. Once all yuca is cooked, transfer fries to bowl of seasoning sprinkle and toss to coat. Alternatively, if batches are small, toss each batch as it's cooked and drained. Serve hot with dipping sauce.

For hints on working with yuca, see p. 88.

Makes 2 servings

10 oz (300 g) yuca, peeled and cut into fries about 3-in (8-cm) long and 1/4–1/2-in (6–8-mm) wide

5 cups (1.25 L) neutral-flavored cooking oil for frying or for a depth of 3-in (8-cm) in pot

Seasoning Sprinkle
1 tsp salt
1 tsp lime zest
1/4 tsp ground cumin
1/4 tsp freshly ground black pepper

Fruited Spicy Dipping Sauce
2 tbsp Rutabaga Pizza / Pasta Sauce (p. 186) or tomato sauce
1 tbsp orange juice
1 tbsp lime juice
1 tbsp apricot jam
1 tsp agave syrup
1/2–1 tsp hot sauce, such as Sriracha, to taste

Truly Hearty Entrées

By transforming recognizable dishes into something new that still provides expected flavors, this collection of recipes is an adventure in creativity. In this chapter, I have pushed both the limits and conceptions of a root vegetable dish while still including homey comfort classics.

Sweet Potato & Pinto Bean Enchiladas

The filling for this Tex–Mex-inspired main is enhanced with a warming spice that isn't spicy. The ever-so-slightly sweet of the potatoes combines with the heat in the chipotle sauce. Satisfying— especially when served with Avocado & Jicama Pico de Gallo (p. 196), Radish & Daikon Pickle (p. 199), or vegan sour cream.

In a large frying pan on medium, toast cumin, coriander, and anise seeds for 2 minutes, until fragrant. Let cool, then grind in spice grinder or food processor.

In same frying pan, heat oil. Add onions and bell peppers. Sauté for 5 minutes, until softened. Add toasted spices, salt, paprika, and ground black pepper. Stir to combine. Add sweet potatoes and 6 tbsp water. Stir, cover, and cook for 8–10 minutes, until potatoes are tender.

Remove from heat and roughly mash to slightly break up sweet potato pieces. Then stir in pinto beans and lime juice and mix well. Taste and adjust seasoning as desired.

Preheat oven to 400°F (200°C). Spray 13 x 9-in (32 x 22-cm) baking dish with non-stick spray.

In a large sauté pan on medium heat, combine tomato sauce, chipotle, cumin, oregano, coriander, and cilantro. Cook for 5 minutes to develop flavors. Reduce heat to low.

Using tongs, soften a tortilla in sauce for 10–20 seconds, turning to coat each side. Using tongs, transfer soaked tortilla to large flat plate. Spread a generous ⅓ cup (80 mL) filling across center of tortilla. Roll up and put, seam side down, into prepared dish. Repeat until dish is filled with two rows of enchiladas.

Add ¼ cup (60 mL) water to thin sauce remaining in pan. Stir to combine. Pour over rolled enchiladas, spreading sauce evenly.

Cover dish with aluminum foil and bake for 30–35 minutes, until steaming hot and tortillas are tender. Remove from oven and uncover. Sprinkle with vegan cheese if using and broil for 2 minutes, until cheese is melted and bubbly. Let sit for 5 minutes before serving to make removal from baking dish easier.

Makes 10 enchiladas

Sweet Potato & Pinto Bean Filling

1 tsp cumin seeds

1 tsp coriander seeds

1/4 tsp anise seeds

1 tbsp olive oil

1/2 medium red onion, diced

1/2 medium green bell pepper, diced

1/2 medium red bell pepper, diced

1/2 tsp salt

1/4 tsp smoked paprika

1/8 tsp freshly ground black pepper

2 1/2–3 cups (625–750 mL) peeled and finely diced white-fleshed sweet potatoes

1 1/2 cups (375 mL) cooked pinto beans, drained, rinsed, and roughly mashed

1 tbsp fresh lime juice

continued

Chipotle Rutabaga Sauce

2 1/2 cups (625 mL) Rutabaga Pizza / Pasta
   Sauce (p. 186) or tomato sauce of choice
1 chipotle, minced (seeding optional)
1 tsp ground cumin
1/2 tsp dried oregano
1/2 tsp ground coriander
1/4 cup (60 mL) finely chopped cilantro

10 5-in (12-cm) corn tortillas

1/2 cup (125 mL) vegan cheese (optional)

Make filling in advance and keep in refrigerator for up to 3 days. Add 10 minutes to cooking time to ensure filling is piping hot.

Potato, Sauerkraut & Dill Pierogies

This dish looks like a huge undertaking, but it really isn't. With a little advance planning (baking the potatoes) and multitasking (resting the dough while you make the filling), you can serve a perfectly plentiful pile of pillowy pierogies for dinner tonight, and put some in the freezer for another day.

Preheat oven to 400°F (200°C).

Prick potatoes with a fork and bake for 75 minutes, until tender. Set aside for 20 minutes, until cool enough to handle. Halve potatoes and scoop out 2 ¼ cups (530 mL) flesh into bowl. Mash and set aside.

While potatoes bake, make dough and filling.

Make dough

In a large bowl, whisk together flours and salt. Form a well. Add 1 ¼ cups (310 mL) water and melted margarine to well and mix with your hands to form a ball of dough.

On a clean floured surface, turn out dough and knead for 3 minutes, until soft, smooth, and elastic. Add more flour as necessary to prevent sticking. Return dough to bowl, cover with plastic wrap, and let dough rest for at least 30 minutes.

Make filling

In a large frying pan on medium, heat margarine and oil. Sauté onions, stirring frequently for 25 minutes, until golden brown with darker brown spots and reduced by three-quarters in volume. Don't let them burn.

Transfer a heaping ½ cup (125 mL) of onions to bowl with mashed potato. Set aside remaining heaping ½ cup (125-mL) in a small bowl to cool. When onions are cool, stir in sour cream and set aside.

To potato-onion mixture, add sauerkraut, dill, salt, and pepper. Mix well.

Makes 45 pierogies

3 medium Russet potatoes

Dough
2 cups (500 mL) all-purpose flour
1/2 cup (125 mL) potato flour
1/2 tsp salt

1/4 cup (60 mL) melted vegan margarine

Filling
1 tbsp vegan margarine
1 tbsp olive oil
4 cups (1 L) sweet onions, such as Walla Walla or Vidalia, finely chopped

3/4 cup (175 mL) vegan sour cream, store-bought or homemade

3/4 cup (175 mL) drained and finely chopped white sauerkraut
2 tbsp finely chopped fresh dill
1/2 tsp salt
1/8 tsp freshly ground pepper

1 tbsp vegan margarine
1 tbsp olive oil

continued

↪ Make pierogies

Sprinkle flour on a large plate and set to one side. On a clean floured board, turn out dough and roll $\frac{1}{16}$-in (1.5-mm) thick. Using a 3-in (8-cm) round cookie cutter, cut out circles of dough, gathering scraps and re-rolling as required. (You should get about 45.)

Gently stretch each circle to a 4-in (10-cm) diameter. The dough should stretch easily without tearing. Place a scant table-spoon of filling in center of dough circle and fold dough over filling, stretching it slightly as required and ensuring there are no air pockets. Pinch to seal.

Place prepared pierogi on floured plate, and dust lightly with flour to prevent pierogies from sticking and drying out. Continue filling dough circles until all are filled, and filling is used up. Let pierogies rest for 20 minutes. Pierogies can be frozen at this point and cooked from frozen later.

Bring a large pot of salted water to a boil. Add pierogies in 2–3 batches (depending on size of pot) and boil for 2–3 minutes, until pierogies rise naturally to surface. (This will take longer if cooking frozen pierogies.) Remove from water with a slotted spoon and allow to drain.

In a large frying pan on medium-high, heat 1 tsp margarine and 1 tsp oil. Fry cooked pierogies in batches, 1–2 minutes per side, until they have a crisp and golden crust. Turn only once. Serve with caramelized onion sour cream.

Reserve the skins from the baked potatoes to make Potato Skins (p. 108).
 Feel free to skip frying the pierogies if you don't like them that way.
 The boiling and frying can be done simultaneously. After boiling the first batch and putting them in the frying pan, start boiling the next batch.

Potato Gnocchi

This cream sauce is intense with garlic. If you're not a garlic fan, use your favorite marinara sauce (or Rutabaga Pizza/Pasta Sauce, p. 186).

Preheat oven to 400°F (200°C).

Slice tops off garlic heads and wrap heads in aluminum foil. Scrub potatoes, prick with fork, and wrap individually in foil. Bake garlic for 30 minutes, until soft and golden, and bake potatoes for 75 minutes, until perfectly tender.

Once garlic is cool enough to handle, squeeze garlic from skins into a small bowl, mash to a paste and set aside for making sauce.

When cool enough to handle, scoop 2 cups (500 mL) potato flesh into a large bowl and mash until no lumps remain. Add flour, semolina, and salt, using your hands to combine. Turn dough onto a clean, lightly floured work surface, and knead for 2–3 minutes to combine well and make dough smooth. Sprinkle work surface with more flour as required to stop sticking.

Divide dough in half. Lightly flour a large plate and set aside. Using your hands, roll each half into a long ½-in (1-cm) diameter rope. Cut each rope into ¾-in (2-cm) pieces. Working with one piece at a time, gently press back of a fork into each piece. Roll off fork to create a small folded dumpling (gnocchi) with indentations. Place on a lightly floured plate until all dough is used. Let gnocchi rest while preparing sauce.

Bring a large pot of salted water to a boil.

In a large frying pan on medium, heat oil. Sauté shallots and garlic for 1 minute, until soft and fragrant. Stir in roasted garlic paste, nutritional yeast, salt, and pepper. Cook for 30 seconds. Add coconut milk, reduce heat to medium-low, and simmer for 5 minutes, until reduced and thickened. Keep on low while gnocchi cook.

Makes 2–4 servings

2 heads garlic, papery skins removed
2 large Russet potatoes

3/4 cup (175 mL) all-purpose flour
3/4 cup (175 mL) durum wheat semolina
1/2 tsp salt

1 tbsp olive oil

1 shallot, minced
1 garlic clove, minced

1 tbsp nutritional yeast
1/2 tsp salt
1/8 tsp freshly ground black pepper

1 cup (250 mL) canned coconut milk

continued

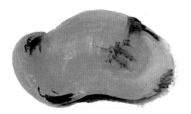

Add gnocchi to boiling water. Stir once with a wooden spoon to ensure they do not stick. Cook until water returns to a full boil and gnocchi have all floated to the surface, about 4 minutes. Drain and add gnocchi to sauce in frying pan. Cook on medium for 1 minute to fully coat with sauce.

Don't make the gnocchi bigger than indicated, or they won't cook evenly.
Reserve the skins from potatoes to make Potato Skins (p. 108).
For a burst of color, toss a handful of spinach or chopped roasted red bell peppers into the sauce just before serving.

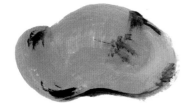

Carrot & Walnut Ravioli with Carrot Top Pesto

Making your own pasta can involve a steep learning curve, but it's rewarding, and once you get the hang of it, you'll have pasta more delicious than anything from a store. Serve these savory nutty delights with Carrot Top Pesto as is or mixed with a little vegan sour cream for a pesto cream sauce.

Make pesto

In a blender or food processor, purée all pesto ingredients until thick and smooth, stopping to scrape down sides of bowl as required. For a thinner consistency, add water 1 tsp at a time, blending after each addition until desired consistency is reached.

Taste and adjust seasoning as desired. Refrigerate until needed.

Make pasta

In a large bowl, whisk together semolina, flour, and salt. Make a well. Add oil and ¼ cup (60 mL) water to well and mix with hands to form a stiff dough. Turn dough out onto clean workstation that is lightly dusted with semolina.

Knead for 10 minutes, until elastic and smooth. The dough will be firmer than bread dough. Wrap in plastic wrap and let rest at room temperature for 20–30 minutes while you prepare filling.

Make filling

In a large frying pan on medium, heat oil. Sauté shallots and carrots for 5 minutes, until soft. Add ¾ cup (175 mL) water, vinegar, salt, thyme, oregano, and pepper. Cook and stir for 5 minutes, until carrots are very soft and most of the liquid has evaporated.

Remove from heat and transfer to a food processor. Purée until smooth, then add walnut crumbs and pulse to combine. Taste and adjust seasoning as desired. Let cool for 5 minutes.

Makes 12

Pesto

1/2 cup (125 mL) tightly packed carrot top leaves, washed thoroughly and stems removed

1/2 cup (125 mL) packed fresh basil leaves

1/2 cup (125 mL) pine nuts, toasted

1/4 cup (60 mL) olive oil

2 tbsp nutritional yeast

1/2 tsp garlic powder

1/4 tsp salt

1/8 tsp freshly ground black pepper

Pasta

1/2 cup (125 mL) durum wheat semolina

1/2 cup (125 mL) all-purpose flour

pinch salt

1 tbsp olive oil

continued

↳ Make ravioli

On a clean workstation dusted with semolina, roll dough by hand or using a pasta rolling machine into a 2-ft (60-cm) long, 6-in (15-cm) wide strip.

Imagine a center line along the length of dough. This is where you'll fold the dough over the filling. Place 1 tbsp filling ½ in (1 cm) from one end of dough and ½ in (1 cm) below imaginary center line. Make 12 1-tbsp mounds of filling along length of dough.

With a pastry brush, brush water on dough between each mound of filling and to edge on half with filling. Fold dough over filling along imaginary line, pressing to seal along fold, as well as between filling to form individual ravioli.

Cut ravioli midway between each mound of filling. Inspect each 3 x 3-in (8 x 8-cm) parcel to ensure it is completely sealed. Lightly dust with semolina and let rest.

Meanwhile, bring a large pot of salted water to a rolling boil. Carefully add ravioli. When ravioli float to the surface, cook for 1 minute. Drain carefully or remove ravioli with a slotted spoon. Toss with pesto.

Use a pasta roller machine or a rolling pin. The dough is strong and will stretch with encouragement. Try to roll it thinly or the cooked pasta may be heavy and stodgy.

You can roll out the pasta and cut any shape you desire. Leave it in large sheets for lasagne.

Durum wheat semolina is also used to make Potato Gnocchi (p. 149).

Filling

1 tbsp olive oil

1 shallot, finely chopped
2 medium carrots, grated

1 tbsp red wine vinegar
1/2 tsp salt
1/4 tsp dried thyme
1/4 tsp dried oregano
1/8 tsp freshly ground black pepper

1/2 cup (125 mL) walnut pieces, pulsed
   to crumbs in a food processor or spice
   grinder

Tunisian-Style Braise with Couscous 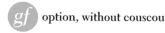 option, without couscous

Serve this wonderfully warming meal family-style: put the big bowl of stew alongside couscous with leftover harissa on the side, and let everyone serve themselves.

Makes 2–4 servings

Harissa
1 tbsp red chile flakes

2 tbsp coriander seeds
1 tbsp cumin seeds

1/2 cup (125 mL) red bell pepper, roasted, seeded and roughly chopped
2 garlic cloves, peeled and crushed
2 tbsp olive oil
1 tbsp lemon juice
1 tsp smoked paprika
1/2 tsp salt

Braise
1 tsp olive oil
1 shallot, finely chopped
1/4 cup (60 mL) finely chopped cilantro stems
1 celery stalk, finely chopped

1/4 tsp turmeric
1/4 tsp ground cinnamon
1/16 tsp ground cloves

5 cups (1.25 L) vegetable stock, divided

Make harissa

In a small bowl, soak chile flakes in 6 tbsp boiling water, covered, for 10 minutes. Drain, discard liquid, and place softened chile flakes in food processor.

In a medium frying pan on medium heat, toast coriander and cumin seeds for 4 minutes, until darkened slightly and fragrant. Remove from heat, cool 5 minutes, and grind to a powder in a spice grinder or food processor. Place ground spices into food processor with soft chile flakes.

To food processor, add bell peppers, garlic, olive oil, lemon juice, paprika, and salt. Blend until smooth and thick. Transfer to a small bowl.

Preheat oven to 375°F (190°C). Have ready a large 9 x 13-in (3.5L) casserole dish.

In a large frying pan, or stovetop-safe casserole, on medium, heat oil. Sauté shallots, cilantro, and celery for 4 minutes until soft. Add 2 tbsp harissa paste, turmeric, cinnamon, and cloves. Sauté for 30 seconds. Deglaze pan with 2 cups (500 mL) stock. Transfer contents to casserole dish. Stir in remaining stock, and add carrots, parsnips, daikon, chickpeas, and raisins.

Cover and bake for 45 minutes. Remove from oven, stir, and return to oven. Bake for 45 more minutes, until vegetables are perfectly tender.

In a medium bowl, place dry couscous. Remove casserole from oven, carefully remove 1 ½ cups (375 mL) cooking stock (leaving some aromatics and chickpeas in the liquid is fine) and add to couscous. Cover bowl and let sit for 5 minutes, until couscous is tender. Fluff with fork before serving.

If you love heat, increase harissa from 2 to 3 tbsp. Although harissa is usually made with whole dried chilies, I've used chile flakes, which are easy to find, in my version of the North African sauce staple.

Use turnip if daikon isn't available. Use the same weight called for in the recipe. Peel and cut into strips the same size and shape as the carrots.

If you have leftover harissa, here are a few suggestions:

- *Stir by the teaspoon into soups and stews to add spice and heat.*

- *Use as a marinade for tofu or tempeh.*

- *Dilute with water or stock and use as a stirfry sauce.*

2 medium carrots, peeled, halved widthwise, then quartered lengthwise

2 medium parsnips, peeled and cut into sticks of equal width and length

4-in (10-cm) length daikon, peeled, cut into 8 wedges

1 1/2 cups (375 mL) cooked chickpeas, drained and rinsed

2 tbsp golden raisins or sultanas

1 cup (250 mL) dry couscous (optional; use 1 cup [250 mL] less stock if omitted)

Parsnip & Spinach Burgers gf

Flecked with green, these naturally sweet burgers crisp well and are best served on soft buns with tomato, avocado, and raw spinach leaves.

In a medium saucepan, combine stock, parsnips, onions, rice, bay leaf, salt, and pepper. The liquid should just about cover all ingredients. Bring to a boil, reduce heat to medium low, cover, and simmer for 45 minutes, until liquid is absorbed and rice is cooked. Spread in a single layer on a large plate and refrigerate for 10 minutes.

In a large bowl, combine ground flaxseeds with 3 tbsp water to make a thick paste. Add mustard, garlic powder, parsley, thyme, sage, celery salt, rosemary, salt, and pepper. Mix to combine.

Add parsnip mixture to seasoned flaxseed paste and mix well. Stir in spinach and rice flour to combine. Mixture will be sticky. With damp hands, form mix into 6 equal-sized burger patties, about 2 in (5 cm) in diameter. Chill formed patties for at least 1 hour for best cooking results.

In a heavy frying pan on medium, heat oil. Carefully place patties into pan and cook for 4–5 minutes per side, until golden brown and crisp.

The patties are a little delicate when newly formed. They will firm up in the refrigerator as the mixture sets but will remain less sturdy than commercially prepared patties.

Makes 6 patties

1 1/2 cups (375 mL) vegetable stock

1 1/2 cups (375 mL) grated parsnips

1/2 onion, grated

1/2 cup (125 mL) short grain brown rice, rinsed

1 bay leaf

pinch each salt and freshly ground black pepper

2 tbsp ground flaxseeds

1/2 tsp Dijon mustard

1/2 tsp garlic powder

1/2 tsp dried parsley

1/4 tsp dried thyme

1/4 tsp dried sage

1/4 tsp celery salt

1/4 tsp dried rosemary

1/4 tsp salt

1/4 tsp freshly ground black pepper

1 cup (250 mL) spinach, stemmed and leaves finely chopped

1/4 cup (60 mL) + 1 tbsp rice flour

1 tbsp olive oil

Kohlrabi & Chickpea Burgers *gf*

The smoky heat of Chipotle Tahini Sauce enhances the natural sweetness and subtle nuttiness of kohlrabi. I love these served on hearty buns with an additional garnish of lettuce and tomato.

Makes 4

Patties

1 tbsp olive oil

1 cup (250 mL) peeled and diced kohlrabi

2 shallots, finely chopped

2 garlic cloves, finely chopped

1 jalapeño, seeded and finely chopped

1 cup (250 mL) cooked chickpeas, drained and rinsed

1/2 cup (125 mL) packed flat-leaf parsley, roughly chopped

1 tsp ground cumin

1/2 tsp onion powder

1/2 tsp salt

1/4 tsp freshly ground black pepper

Chipotle Tahini Sauce

2 tbsp tahini

1 tsp minced chipotle in adobo

1/2 tsp flaxseed oil

1/2 tsp lemon juice

1/8 tsp garlic powder

pinch each salt and freshly ground black pepper

1 tbsp olive oil

In a medium frying pan on medium, heat oil and add kohlrabi. Cover and cook, stirring occasionally, for 6–8 minutes, until tender and browned. Add shallots, garlic, and jalapeño, and sauté for 2 minutes, until softened and fragrant. Remove from heat and transfer to a food processor.

Add chickpeas, parsley, cumin, onion powder, salt, and pepper. Pulse to combine, breaking up chickpeas and kohlrabi until no large pieces remain. Do not process until completely smooth, as you want a little texture. The mix should hold together easily if pressed.

Using a 1/3 cup (80 mL) measuring cup, scoop mixture and shape into patties. Chill for an hour at this point for best results.

While mixture chills, make sauce.

Make sauce

In a medium bowl, whisk together all sauce ingredients. Thin with 2 tbsp water to achieve desired consistency. Cover and set aside in refrigerator.

In a large frying pan on medium, heat oil. Cook patties for 3–4 minutes, until browned and crispy, then flip and cook for 3 more minutes.

As patties fry, prepare garnish.

Make garnish

In a second large frying pan, heat oil on medium-high. Add shallots and seasonings and sauté for 2 minutes, until browned. Add greens and sauté for 2 minutes, until wilted. Add 2 tbsp water and cook 1 minute, until further softened and liquid has evaporated.

Serve burgers with prepared sauce and topped with garnish.

This recipe calls for kohlrabi greens. These tasty leaves are akin to kale or collard greens in texture, which you can use instead, or use an equal amount of turnip or rutabaga greens.

Kohlrabi Greens Garnish

1 tbsp olive oil

1 small shallot, halved and thinly sliced
pinch each salt and pepper

1 cup (250 mL) shredded kohlrabi greens,
  thick stems removed

Parsnip & Pea Risotto gf

The natural sweetness of parsnips is highlighted by the grassy intensity of tarragon and sauvignon blanc. Rich and filling, this is a dish to savor with a glass of wine from the bottle you cooked with and a crusty loaf of sourdough bread.

Makes 4 servings

1 tbsp olive oil
3 medium parsnips, peeled and diced

1/4 cup (60 mL) nutritional yeast
1/4 cup (60 mL) hemp seeds
1/4 cup (60 mL) + 2 tbsp unsweetened
   nondairy milk

2 tbsp olive oil
2 shallots, finely chopped
1 celery stalk, finely chopped

1 tsp dried tarragon
1 1/2 cups (375 mL) arborio (risotto) rice

1/2 cup (125 mL) sauvignon blanc, other
   white wine, or vegetable stock

5 cups (1.25 L) vegetable stock

1 1/2 cups (375 mL) thawed frozen peas

salt and pepper, to taste
fresh tarragon, for garnish (optional)

In a large saucepan on medium-high, heat 1 tbsp oil. Add parsnips and sauté for 5 minutes, until golden and just tender. Remove from heat and reserve half of parsnips. Place other half in blender or food processor. Add yeast, hemp seeds, and milk. Blend to form a smooth thick paste. Set aside.

In same saucepan on medium, heat 2 tbsp oil. Sauté shallots and celery for 5 minutes, until soft and lightly browned. Add tarragon and rice. Toast for 2 minutes, stirring frequently, until very fragrant. Deglaze pan with wine for 1 minute, until absorbed by rice.

Add reserved parsnip. Add stock ½ cup (125 mL) at a time, stirring after each addition and more frequently as stock is absorbed by rice. Once stock is fully absorbed, add more, and repeat until all stock has been added and last addition is nearly absorbed, 18–20 minutes. Rice should be tender yet firm, and the risotto should be loose.

Stir in parsnip paste to dissolve and thicken, about 2 minutes. Stir in peas and heat through for about 2 minutes. Taste and adjust seasoning as desired. Garnish with tarragon leaves.

Sunchoke Falafel gf

In this recipe, chickpeas are gently augmented in order to appreciate their slight nuttiness, though these still bring traditional falafel to mind. The tahini sauce puts a chees-y spin on the usual accompaniment. You'll have enough for 6 sandwiches.

Make sauce

In a small bowl, whisk together all ingredients with 3 tbsp water until smooth. Chill until required. Makes scant ⅔ cup.

Make falafel

In a food processor, combine sunchokes, chickpeas, parsley, garlic, onions, and lemon juice. Pulse to break up whole chickpeas and herbs.

Add tahini, lemon juice and zest, salt, cumin, coriander, black pepper, and cayenne. Pulse to combine to form a thick chunky paste. Do not over process, as mix should not be smooth.

Scoop mixture by the tablespoon to form into balls if deep frying, or into 1-in (2.5-cm) discs if baking or shallow frying.

Cook falafel using preferred method:

Bake falafel

Preheat oven to 400°F (200°C). Line a baking sheet with parchment paper. Place discs onto prepared sheet. Bake for 10 minutes, carefully turn, and bake for 10 more minutes, until firm and both sides are golden brown.

Deep-fry falafel

In a large pot on medium, heat 2–3 in (5–8 cm) neutral-flavored oil to 375°F (190°C) on a deep-fry thermometer, or so that a small piece of falafel dropped into hot oil immediately sizzles vigorously. Line a large plate with paper towels.

Add falafel balls to hot oil, working in batches and taking care not to overcrowd pot. Cook for 1 minute until golden brown and crisp. Drain on paper towels.

Makes 24 falafel

Sauce

3 tbsp canned coconut milk

2 tbsp tahini or sunflower seed butter

2 tbsp nutritional yeast

1/2 tsp ground cumin

1/4 tsp salt

1/8 tsp freshly ground black pepper

1/8 tsp turmeric

1/8 tsp dried mustard

1/8 tsp black salt

Falafel

1 1/4 cups (310 mL) scrubbed and grated sunchokes

1 1/4 cups (310 mL) cooked chickpeas, drained and rinsed

1/4 cup (60 mL) loosely packed flat-leaf parsley

1 garlic clove

3 spring onions, roughly chopped

1 tbsp lemon juice

2 tbsp tahini or sunflower seed butter

1 tbsp fresh lemon juice

1 tsp lemon zest

1/2 tsp salt

1/4 tsp ground cumin

1/4 tsp ground coriander

1/8 tsp freshly ground black pepper

pinch cayenne

continued

↳ for deep frying: 5 cups (1.25 L) neutral-
flavored oil or enough for 2–3-in (5–8-cm)
in pot
for shallow frying: 1 tbsp olive oil

To serve
6 soft flat pita breads (or serve over cooked
rice for GF option)
1 1/2 cups (375 mL) shredded lettuce
2 tomatoes, sliced
3 spring onions, thinly sliced on the bias
1/2 medium red bell pepper, seeded and
thinly sliced
18 slices cucumber

Shallow-fry falafel

In a large frying pan on medium, heat oil. Add falafel patties, frying in batches and taking care not to overcrowd pan. Fry for 2 minutes, turn carefully, and fry for another 2 minutes, until golden brown and crusty.

Assemble sandwiches

Spread 1 tbsp sauce on each pita. Place ¼ cup (60 mL) shredded lettuce across center of each pita, top with tomatoes, onions, bell peppers, and cucumber. Fold in sides of pita to form sandwich.

Here are three options for cooking:

- *Baking: contains no oil. Falafel will be more dry than if fried, but not overly so. A little delicate to turn.*
- *Deep-fried: traditional. Can be formed into balls, which fall apart with the other two methods. Crispy outside and soft inside.*
- *Shallow-fried: combo of the above methods. You get crunch and a crust on the outside, but they're a little delicate to turn.*

Ground Beet Tacos gf

For those who like taco fillings without beans, this is a rich and thick savory "meat-y" option.
Be sure to top the tacos with lots of lettuce, tomato, and some Radish & Carrot Citrus Slaw (p. 102).

In a dry frying pan on medium, toast cumin seeds, fennel seeds, chile flakes, cumin, and coriander until fragrant, taking care not to burn, for about 2 minutes. Transfer to slow cooker.

Add beets, TVP, onions, garlic, jalapeño pepper, tomato paste, liquid smoke, Marmite, hot sauce, salt, pepper, tomato juice, and stock to slow cooker. Stir to combine well. Cover and cook on low setting for 6 hours, until tender and thick. Season with salt, pepper, and hot sauce, as desired.

In a large frying pan on medium, heat corn tortillas for 30 seconds on each side until pliable.

Place 2–4 tbsp beet filling in center of each tortilla, and top with tomato slices, shredded lettuce, slaw, and pico de gallo.

This filling is quite moist. If you prefer a drier filling, after 6 hours cooking time, turn slow cooker to high and cook, uncovered, for 1 hour, stirring occasionally to allow some liquid to evaporate.

Makes 4–6 servings

Note: Slow cooker needed

1 tsp cumin seeds
1/2 tsp ground fennel seeds
1/2 tsp chile flakes, more to taste
1 tsp ground cumin
1 tsp ground coriander

1 1/4 cups (310 mL) grated beets
1 1/2 cups (375 mL) TVP granules
1/2 red onion, finely chopped
3 garlic cloves, minced
1 jalapeño or serrano pepper, minced
1 1/2 tbsp tomato paste
2 tsp liquid smoke
2 tsp Marmite or soy sauce
1/2–1 tsp hot sauce to taste (optional)
3/4 tsp salt
1/2 tsp freshly ground black pepper
1 1/2 cups (375 mL) tomato juice
1 1/4 cups (310 mL) vegetable stock

salt, pepper, and additional hot sauce to taste

8–12 6-in (15-cm) corn tortillas
1–2 medium tomatoes, thinly sliced
2 cups (500 mL) shredded lettuce
1 cup (250 mL) Radish & Carrot Citrus Slaw (p. 102) or your favorite
1/2 cup (125 mL) Avocado & Jicama Pico de Gallo (p. 196)

Yuca Empanadas with Avocado, Plantain & Black Beans

The final result is worth all the steps involved to bring this dish together. Subtly spicy and enhanced with different textures, these savory South American-inspired parcels can be enjoyed hot or cold.

Prepare yuca

Bring a medium saucepan of water to a boil. Add yuca pieces and return water to a boil. Cook for 10 minutes, until yuca is tender and translucent. Drain and discard cooking water. Rinse yuca under cold water and drain again. Set aside.

Make dough

In a small bowl, mix ¾ cup (175 mL) + 3 tbsp water and lime juice. Chill in freezer for 10 minutes. While yuca is boiling, in a large bowl whisk together flours, salt, paprika, and black pepper. Rub in cold shortening to form crumbs. Add chilled lime-water mixture. Mix with hands to combine and form a dough. Knead lightly for 1 minute to fully combine. Wrap in plastic wrap and let rest at room temperature for at least 30 minutes.

Prepare filling

In a small bowl, mix cilantro, cubed avocados, and lime juice. Toss to combine. Set aside.

In a small bowl, mash half the beans until smooth. Fold in remaining whole beans and set aside.

In a large frying pan on medium-high, heat oil. Line a plate with paper towels. Fry plantain pieces, stirring frequently, until golden brown, about for 4 minutes. Drain on paper towels, then transfer to a large bowl and set aside.

In same hot frying pan and oil, reduce heat to medium and sauté onions and bell peppers for 5 minutes, until softened and starting to brown. Stir in serrano, garlic, paprika, coriander, cumin, salt, and pepper and sauté for 2 minutes. Add tomato juice, syrup, and hot sauce. Stir to combine well.

Makes 18 empanadas

1 1/2 cups (375 mL) peeled and diced yuca

Dough
3 tbsp lime juice
3 cups (750 mL) all-purpose flour
3/4 cup (175 mL) potato flour
1 1/2 tsp salt
3/4 tsp smoked paprika
1/4 tsp freshly ground black pepper

3/4 cup (175 mL) vegan shortening, chilled

Filling
1/4 cup (60 mL) finely chopped cilantro
1 ripe avocado, peeled, pitted, and cubed
1 tbsp lime juice

1 1/2 cups (375 mL) cooked black beans,
  drained and rinsed

1/4 cup (60 mL) neutral-flavored oil
1 medium green plantain, peeled and diced

1 onion, finely chopped
1/2 green bell pepper, finely chopped

continued

↳ 1 serrano or jalapeño pepper, minced
   (seeding optional)

2 garlic cloves

1 tsp smoked paprika

1 tsp ground coriander

1/2 tsp ground cumin

1/2 tsp salt

1/4 tsp freshly ground black pepper

2 cups (500 mL) tomato juice

1 tsp agave syrup

1/2 tsp hot sauce

Add cooked yuca and whole and mashed beans. Cook, stirring occasionally, until liquid is reduced and mixture is thickened, about 10 minutes. Let cool as dough rests and oven heats.

Make empanadas

Preheat oven to 400°F (200°C). Line a large baking sheet with parchment paper.

To bowl containing plantain, add yuca-bean filling and avocado-cilantro mix. Stir gently to combine. Taste and adjust seasoning as desired.

Remove 3 oz (90 g) of dough. Keep remaining dough covered to prevent drying.

Using a rolling pin, roll dough into a rough 8-in (20-cm) circle. Place ¼ cup (60 mL) filling in center of circle. Bring 2 sides of circle to meet evenly above filling. Pinch to seal dough just above filling.

Starting at one end, roll top seal of dough under to form a rope-like seal, working toward opposite end. Pinch off and remove any excess dough.

Place finished empanada on prepared baking sheet and cover with a clean tea towel. Continue to shape and fill empanadas until dough and filling are used up.

With a sharp knife, poke a small slit in each empanada to allow steam to escape. Bake for 25 minutes, until golden brown and filling is piping hot.

For hints on using yuca, see p. 88.

The yuca filling can be prepared in advance and kept in the refrigerator for up to 2 days.

If making fillings in advance, prepare each and set aside until just before using to maintain textural differences as much as possible.

Celeriac-Stuffed Portobello Mushrooms option

This is what I'll be serving for Thanksgiving dinner in our house this year (and potentially every year). The mushrooms are perfectly moist and tender and complement the savory celeriac stuffing. The best word to describe the accompanying reduction is intense; it's a little sweet with a hint of sour and notes of wine, beets, and vinegar. Only a little is needed to add punch.

Makes 4 servings

Note: Juicer needed to make reduction

Beet & Balsamic Reduction

1 lb (500 g) beets, peeled if not organic

1 cup (250 mL) red wine, such as merlot
6 tbsp balsamic vinegar
2 tsp brown rice syrup
1 tsp garlic powder
1 tsp onion powder

Stuffed mushrooms

4 large Portobello caps, wiped clean, stalks
   and gills removed
pinch each salt and freshly ground black
   pepper

Make reduction

In a juicer, juice beets.

In a medium saucepan, combine 1 cup (250 mL) beet juice with wine, vinegar, syrup, garlic powder, and onion powder.

Bring to a boil. Reduce heat to medium and simmer for 20–22 minutes, stirring constantly for the last 3–4 minutes to ensure mixture doesn't burn. You will be left with about ⅓ cup (80-mL) thick, syrupy sauce. As reduction cooks down, make stuffed mushrooms.

Make stuffed mushrooms

Preheat oven to 400°F (200°C).

Place mushrooms gill cavity side up in a large roasting pan. Place 2 tbsp water in bottom of pan, season mushrooms with salt and pepper, and cover with foil.

Bake for 25 minutes, until mushrooms are just tender. While mushrooms bake, prepare filling.

Make filling

In a small bowl, whisk together ground flaxseeds and 7 tbsp water.

In a large frying pan on medium, heat oil. Sauté shallots, garlic, and celeriac for 7 minutes, until very soft, lightly browned, and reduced by half in volume. Add sage, salt, and pepper, and sauté for 30 seconds more. Remove from heat and transfer to a large bowl.

To bowl, add ground almonds, breadcrumbs, chives, and yeast. Mix to combine. Stir in soaked flaxseeds. The mixture will be damp but not wet to touch, and will hold together when pressed.

Remove mushrooms from oven, uncover, and use tongs to drain any liquid from inside gill cavities before stuffing.

Place ¼ cup (60 mL) thawed peas in cavity of each mushroom. Scoop ½ packed cup (125 mL) stuffing mix and invert into mushroom cavity so filling is in the shape of a cup in cavity. Press gently on filling so it stays in place.

Bake, uncovered, for 20–25 minutes, until stuffing is lightly browned and firm and mushrooms are completely tender.

Serve drizzled with prepared reduction.

You can make the stuffing and reduction in advance, which will help with planning for the big meal.

As the reduction sits, it may thicken. Add water by the half-teaspoon until you reach desired consistency for drizzling.

Filling

2 tbsp ground flaxseeds

1 tbsp olive oil

1 shallot, finely chopped
2 garlic cloves, minced
2 cups (500 mL) peeled and grated celeriac

1 1/2 tsp dried sage
1/2 tsp salt
1/8 tsp freshly ground black pepper

1/2 cup (125 mL) ground almonds
1/3 cup (80 mL) dry breadcrumbs (can be gluten-free)
2 tbsp chives, finely chopped
1 tbsp nutritional yeast

1 cup (250 mL) thawed frozen peas

Water Chestnut & Chestnut-Stuffed Tofu

Quick, easy, and so impressive. Perhaps the perfect holiday main dish for its ease of execution and interesting flavors and textures. Serve with extra stuffing and gravy glaze on the side. The optional mixed peel adds small bursts of sweetness to the stuffing, so be brave—put it in.

Preheat oven to 400°F (200°C). Have a baking sheet ready. With cooking spray, lightly oil 5 6-in (15-cm) pieces of aluminum foil.

Make stuffing

In a large bowl, soak flaxseeds in 1 ½ tbsp water.

In a medium frying pan on medium-high, heat oil. Sauté celery, shallots, and garlic for 3 minutes, until soft and just starting to brown.

Place cooked vegetables in food processor with water chestnuts, cooked chestnuts, and mixed peel. Pulse until consistency of large breadcrumbs. Transfer to large bowl containing flaxseeds. Add sage, thyme, oregano, salt, pepper, and fennel seeds. Mix to combine well. Taste and adjust seasoning as desired.

Cut pressed tofu in half to form 2 equal-sized cubes, then cut each cube in half through the middle to form 4 square slices. Cut top and 1 side of tofu slices to form pockets, leaving 2 sides uncut. Stuff 1 ½ tbsp stuffing into each pocket. Tuck stuffing into corners but take care not to split sides. Wrap each stuffed tofu in aluminum foil and place on sheet. Wrap leftover stuffing in remaining foil and place on sheet. Bake for 30 minutes until piping hot, tofu is tender, and stuffing is starting to firm.

Make glaze

In a small bowl, whisk together mayonnaise, Marmite, syrup, mustard, and liquid smoke.

Remove tofu and packet of stuffing from oven. Open aluminum foil packets and brush tops of tofu liberally with glaze. Leave packets open and return to oven. Bake for 10 more minutes, until glaze is thickened and sticky, and stuffing in foil packet is firm but still moist.

For information on water chestnuts, see p. 94.

Makes 4 servings

Stuffing
1 tbsp ground flaxseeds

1 tsp olive oil
1 celery stalk, chopped
1 shallot, chopped
1 garlic clove, chopped

1/2 cup (125 mL) peeled and roughly chopped water chestnuts (about 8)
1/2 cup (125 mL) peeled and roughly chopped cooked chestnuts (about 8)
1 tbsp mixed peel (optional)

1/2 tsp dried sage
1/2 tsp dried thyme
1/2 tsp dried oregano
1/2 tsp salt
1/4 tsp freshly ground black pepper
1/8 tsp ground fennel seeds

1 lb (500 g) extra-firm tofu, drained and pressed

Gravy Glaze
1/4 cup (60 mL) Sweet Potato Mayo (p. 192) or your favorite vegan mayonnaise
1 tbsp Marmite
2 tsp brown rice syrup
1 tsp Dijon mustard
2 or 3 drops liquid smoke, to taste

➔ To cook fresh chestnuts

If you're planning to cook fresh chestnuts for the stuffing, here are my recommendations:

- **Cook more than recipe calls for.**

- **Cook them in advance.**

- **Have precooked chestnuts available as a backup, in case some (or all) of your chestnuts have spoiled, which you won't discover until you peel the cooked chestnuts.**

Preheat oven to 400°F (200°C).

With a sharp knife, mark two cuts in the shape of a cross in bulging side of chestnut shell. Place on baking sheet cross side up, and bake for 35–45 minutes, until chestnuts burst from the crossed cuts in shell.

Remove from oven and, wearing an oven mitt, crack open and peel away hot shells to remove the edible nuts.

Golden Chili gf

This hearty, golden-hued dish of beans and TVP is a subtle blend of naturally sweet beets and peppers with the acid hit of tomatoes. Add a second serrano if you like things spicy.

Makes 4 servings

1 cup (250 mL) TVP granules
1 1/4 cups (310 mL) boiling vegetable stock

1 tbsp olive oil
1 medium onion, finely chopped
2 garlic cloves, minced
1 serrano pepper, minced

1 1/2 tbsp tomato paste
1/2 tsp ancho chile powder
1/2 tsp ground cumin
1/2 tsp curry powder
1/2 tsp paprika

1 1/2 cups (375 mL) roasted and roughly
   chopped yellow or orange bell peppers
   (or combination)
1 1/2 cups (375 mL) finely grated golden
   beets

1 1/2 cups (375 mL) canned diced tomatoes
2 cups (500 mL) cooked red kidney beans,
   drained and rinsed
1 cup (250 mL) vegetable stock

salt and freshly ground black pepper to
   taste

In a medium bowl, combine TVP and boiling stock. Cover and let sit for 15 minutes, until liquid is absorbed.

In a large pot on medium, heat oil. Sauté onions, garlic, and serrano pepper for 5 minutes, until soft and onions are translucent. Add tomato paste, chile powder, cumin, curry powder, and paprika. Cook for 1 minute, stirring to coat vegetables. Add bell peppers and beets and cook for 2 minutes, stirring to combine well.

Add TVP, canned tomatoes, kidney beans, and stock. Stir to combine well. Bring to a boil, reduce heat to medium-low, cover, and simmer, stirring occasionally, for 15 minutes, until beets are cooked and flavors have developed.

Increase heat to medium, and cook, uncovered, stirring occasionally, for 10 minutes to reduce liquid and thicken chili. Taste and adjust seasoning as desired.

Turnip Cabbage Rolls _gf_

Maybe not quite like Grandma's. This version has a tasty, lightly spiced filling using turnips and potatoes instead of the traditional rice, because I love the earthy flavor they add.

Preheat oven to 400°F (200°C). Lightly grease a 9 x13-in (3.5 L) casserole or baking dish.

In a medium bowl, combine TVP granules and stock, cover, and let sit for 15 minutes.

Fill a large sauté pan with water and bring to a boil. Using tongs, blanch cabbage leaves, 6 halves at a time, for 30 seconds, or until pliable, turning as necessary. Remove from boiling water and immerse in cold water to stop cooking to retain their bright green color. Once all leaves are blanched, discard water.

In same pan on medium, heat oil. Add onions, turnips, and potatoes. Sauté for 8–10 minutes, until soft, translucent, and reduced by about half in volume. Add both types of paprika, oregano, salt, caraway seeds, black pepper, cayenne, and rehydrated TVP. Sauté for 2 minutes to combine flavors. Stir in parsley and remove from heat.

In prepared casserole dish, combine crushed tomatoes, syrup, vinegar, salt, dill, and paprika.

Divide TVP-turnip filling mix into 12 equal portions, roughly ¼ cup (60 mL) each.

Place ¼ cup (60 mL) filling mixture in center of a blanched half-leaf. Fold two sides toward the center over filling, hold them down, and fold end closest to you over folded cabbage. Then turn roll over to sit on unfolded end (as you would a burrito).

Place filled cabbage roll in sauce in casserole. Repeat with remaining leaves, placing rolls in a single layer. The sauce won't completely cover rolls.

Cover dish with aluminum foil and cook for 40–45 minutes, until cabbage is completely tender and sauce is bubbly and thickened.

Makes 12 cabbage rolls

1 cup (250 mL) TVP granules

1 cup (250 mL) boiling vegetable stock or water

6 large Savoy or green cabbage leaves, thick center spines removed to make 12 halves

1 tbsp olive oil

1 medium onion, finely chopped

1 cup (250 mL) peeled and grated turnips

1 cup (250 mL) peeled and grated Yukon Gold potatoes

1/2 tsp paprika

1/2 tsp smoked paprika

1/2 tsp dried oregano

1/2 tsp salt

1/4 tsp caraway seeds

1/4 tsp freshly ground black pepper

1/8 tsp cayenne (optional), to taste

1/4 cup (60 mL) finely chopped fresh parsley

2 cups (500 mL) canned crushed tomatoes, or 1 1/2 cups (375 mL) Rutabaga Pizza/Pasta Sauce (p. 186) thinned with 1/2 cup (125 mL) vegetable stock or water

1 tbsp agave syrup

1 tsp balsamic vinegar

1/2 tsp salt

1/2 tsp dried dill

1/2 tsp paprika

↱ Buy a big cabbage. Or, if you don't want to eat cabbage for a whole week, have a chat with the produce manager at your store. Mine was quite happy to cut off the outer leaves to sell to me, as these are often discarded.

- To remove leaves from cabbage, cut stalk and peel each leaf up from bottom. Alternately, slice hard center from the leaf while it's still on the head and peel off.

- If cabbage leaves are smaller than about 6 x 5-in (15x 12-cm), use 2 for each cabbage roll. Better to blanch too many than not enough.

- You can skip blanching step by freezing individual cabbage leaves. Prepare as you would for blanching, freeze for 24 hours, then thaw. Once leaves are thawed, they are soft and pliable and cook well.

- Cabbage rolls can be prepared in advance and then refrigerated for up to 24 hours. Bring to room tem-perature before baking, and add 5 minutes to cooking time.

Neep-y Haggis (if using certified gluten-free oats)

Bashed Neeps (mashed rutabaga) is traditionally served with haggis. In this vegan version, it's part of the haggis itself. And in case you were wondering, not all haggis is stuffed into a casing. In Scotland, you'll often find it presented like this.

Preheat oven to 400°F (200°C).

In a large oven-safe pot on medium, melt margarine. Sauté rolled oats, steel-cut oats, and walnuts for 5 minutes, until toasty and golden. Transfer to a large bowl and set aside.

In same pot on medium, heat oil and sauté onions for 5 minutes, until soft and translucent. Add mushrooms and sauté for 5 minutes, until liquid is just released. Add kidney beans and rutabaga, and sauté for 5 minutes to soften.

Add ½ cup (125 mL) stock, whisky, lemon juice, pepper, Marmite, sage, thyme, rosemary, oregano, salt, onion powder, and garlic powder. Stir well. Add toasted oats and nuts to pot and stir to combine well.

Transfer pot to heated oven and bake for 15 minutes. Remove from oven, add ¼ cup (60 mL) stock and stir. Return to oven, and bake for 15 more minutes. Remove from oven, add ¼ cup (60 mL) more stock, and return to oven. Repeat until all stock is added, oats are cooked and a little chewy, haggis is a lovely brown, and a crust has formed at the edge of the pot. Stir. The haggis should be firm but not dry. Add additional ¼ cup (60 mL) stock if haggis looks dry.

Leftovers are good sliced and pan-fried until outsides are a little crispy. It also makes a great fancy dinner wrapped in puff pastry and baked at 400°F (200°C) for 15–20 minutes, until piping hot with a golden brown flaky crust (a little like a Wellington). Just carve and serve.

Makes 4–6 servings

1 tbsp vegan margarine
1/2 cup (125 mL) quick-cooking or old-fashioned rolled oats
1/2 cup (125 mL) steel-cut oats
1/2 cup (125 mL) small walnut pieces

1 tbsp neutral-flavored oil
1 cup (250 mL) finely chopped onions
2 cups (500 mL) finely chopped button mushrooms
1 1/2 cups (375 mL) roughly chopped cooked red kidney beans
1 cup (250 mL) grated rutabaga or carrot

1 1/4 cups (310 mL) vegetable stock, divided, more if required
1/4 cup (60 mL) whisky or stock
2 tbsp lemon juice
1 tsp white pepper
1 tsp Marmite
1 tsp ground dried sage
1 tsp dried thyme
1 tsp dried rosemary
1/2 tsp dried oregano
1/4 tsp salt
1/4 tsp onion powder
1/4 tsp garlic powder

Field & Garden Stew *gf*

When I was growing up, we had a very large garden and grew almost all our own fruit and vegetables, except mushrooms. Luckily for us, our neighbor's farm had wild white mushrooms galore, and I have fond memories of mushrooming with my family. This meal-in-a-bowl incorporates elements from both garden and field.

Makes 4–6 servings

1/4 cup (60 mL) potato flour

2 tbsp potato starch

2 garlic cloves, minced

1 1/2 tsp Marmite or dark miso paste

1 tsp dried thyme

1/4 tsp freshly ground black pepper

1/2 tsp dried rosemary

2 tbsp soy sauce

1/2 cup (125 mL) nondairy milk

2 cups (500 mL) warm mushroom or
  vegetable stock

3 cups (750 mL) diced Yukon Gold
  potatoes (peeling optional)

1/2 cup (125 mL) peeled and diced carrots

3/4 cup (175 mL) peeled and diced turnips

1 celery stalk, finely chopped

1 medium onion, finely chopped

6 medium button mushrooms, cut into
  1/4-in (6-mm) pieces

1 Portobello mushroom, stalk removed, cut
  in 1/4-in (6-mm) pieces

1/2 cup (125 mL) thawed frozen peas

1/2 cup (125 mL) thawed frozen corn kernels

Preheat oven to 400°F (200°C).

In a 9 x 13-in (3.5 L) casserole dish, whisk together potato flour, potato starch, garlic, Marmite, thyme, pepper, rosemary, soy sauce, milk, and stock. Leaving some lumps is fine. Place potatoes in casserole dish. They should be completely covered by liquid.

Add carrots, turnips, celery, onions, and mushrooms in order given. Press gently to submerge vegetables as much as possible. The mushrooms release liquid as they cook.

Cover with aluminum foil or a lid and bake for 55–60 minutes, until all vegetables are just fork tender. Be sure to check that potatoes on bottom layer are cooked.

Add thawed frozen vegetables. Stir and bake, uncovered, for 20 more minutes, until all vegetables are completely tender.

The addition of frozen vegetables is for the gardenless among us. If you have a garden, add an equal amount of finely chopped fresh seasonal vegetables: corn kernels, peas, green beans, broccoli, and cauliflower all work well.

Beer, Onion & Rutabaga Sausage

My take on beer brats, these sausages are slightly sweet and wonderful with a dab of Horseradish Crema (p. 187) for a touch of sour and spicy contrast. I have caramelized the onion the cheater's way to cut down on the preparation time.

Makes 5 sausages

1/2 small rutabaga, peeled and cut into 1/2-in (1-cm) dice

1 tbsp olive oil
1 medium onion, finely chopped
1 1/2 tsp light brown sugar

1 1/4 cups (310 mL) beer, such as a medium-bodied lager, or vegetable stock
3/4 tsp salt
1/4 tsp freshly ground black pepper
1/8 tsp chile flakes
1/8 tsp ground fennel seeds

3/4 cup (175 mL) + 1 tbsp vital wheat gluten
1/4 cup (60 mL) nutritional yeast

In a medium saucepan, cover rutabaga with water. Bring to a boil on high, then reduce heat to medium, and cook for 25 minutes, until very tender. Drain, then transfer to a food processor or blender and process until smooth.

In a large frying pan on medium, heat oil. Sauté onions for 5–7 minutes, until soft and lightly browned. Add brown sugar and cook 3 more minutes to lightly caramelize. Add splashes of water if onions stick. Volume will be reduced by about half.

Add rutabaga purée, beer, salt, black pepper, chile flakes, and fennel seeds to onions. Cook for 2 minutes. Transfer to a large bowl and allow to cool to room temperature, about 30 minutes.

Fit a medium saucepan with a steamer basket. Add water to reach bottom of basket. Have ready 5 6-in (15-cm) pieces of aluminum foil.

Add wheat gluten and nutritional yeast to bowl, and mix to combine well. Knead with hands for 3–4 minutes to activate gluten. The mixture will be quite damp. Divide into five equal pieces and shape into logs about 4 in (10 cm) long and roughly 1 in (2.5 cm) wide. Wrap tightly in aluminum foil, and place in steamer basket.

Cover, bring water to a boil, and reduce heat to medium-low. Simmer for 60 minutes, until sausages are firm to the touch. Check water level periodically and top up as needed. Remove from heat and when sausages are cool enough to handle, remove from foil.

Panfry, grill, or barbeque whole or sliced in half lengthwise. If not cooking immediately, allow to cool fully before refrigerating for up to 3 days.

There are many steps, all of which can be completed in advance — cooking and blending the rutabaga, cooking the onions, and steaming the sausage.

Lotus Root Thai Green Curry gf

A colorful introduction to lotus root, this bowl is a contrast in texture—mild, crunchy cooked lotus root, soft tofu, and tender rice and red bell peppers, a cooling combination that balances the abundance of flavors in the curry paste.

Make curry paste

In a food processor, pulse together cilantro stems, jalapeños, shallot, garlic, ginger, lemongrass, basil leaves, 1 tbsp oil, soy sauce, lime zest and juice, coriander, and cumin until well combined and paste-like, stopping to scrape down sides of bowl as required.

Taste and adjusting seasoning as desired. Store in refrigerator for up to 3 days until needed, if making in advance. Makes just over ½ cup (125 mL).

In a large sauté pan (straight-sided) on medium-high, heat ½ tbsp oil. Sauté tofu for 4–5 minutes, until browned on each side. Remove from pan and drain on paper towels.

In same pan, reduce heat to medium. Add curry paste and sauté for 2 minutes, until very fragrant and green color has deepened. Add tofu and lotus root. Cook for 1 minute, stirring to coat with paste. Add coconut milk and simmer for 10 minutes, until sauce is thickened and reduced. Stir in red bell peppers and cook for 3 minutes, until softened and sauce coats vegetables. The sauce will be thick.

Serve over rice and garnish each bowl with 1 tbsp cilantro leaves.

For information on lotus root, see p. 64.

If you're heat-averse, remove seeds from jalapeños, or reduce to 2. The paste will remain flavorful and well-rounded, just less hot.

Makes 4 servings

Curry Paste

1/4 cup (60 mL) cilantro stems, roughly chopped

3 jalapeños, roughly chopped, seeding optional

1 shallot, roughly chopped

2 garlic cloves, roughly chopped

2 tbsp peeled and roughly chopped ginger

about 1 tbsp roughly chopped soft centers of lemongrass stalks

1 tbsp Thai (or regular) basil leaves

1 tbsp coconut oil

2 tbsp soy sauce

1 tsp lime zest

1 tsp lime juice

1 tsp ground coriander

1 tsp ground cumin

1/2 tbsp coconut oil

6 oz (175 g) extra-firm tofu, drained, pressed for 15 minutes and cut into 1/2-in (1-cm) cubes

5-in (12-cm) length lotus root, quartered and sliced 1/4-in (6-mm) thick, about 1 1/2 cups (375 mL)

1 1/2 cups (375 mL) coconut milk

1/2 red bell pepper, thinly sliced into 1/2-in (1-cm) long strips

4 cups cooked Thai jasmine, white, or brown rice

1/4 cup (60 mL) cilantro leaves

Truly Saucy Condiments

These recipes were created to not only showcase but also complement root vegetables. More than that, condiments add flavor dimensions to any dish. Mix and match as you like, or see my tips on each recipe.

Carrot Peanut Sauce

Perfectly nutty, this slightly spicy sauce gets its hint of sweetness from carrot. Use wherever you'd like a hint of hot or cold peanut goodness—with rice or soba noodles, over green vegetables, or as a salad dressing.

In a medium pan on medium, heat oil. Sauté onions and carrots for 4 minutes until very soft and all liquid has been released and cooked away. Stir in cumin, garlic powder, and chile flakes, and cook for 1 minute. Stir in 6 tbsp water, tomato sauce, soy sauce, hot sauce, and peanut butter. Cook for 2 minutes, until well combined. Remove from heat and stir in lime juice and milk.

With an immersion blender or in a countertop blender, working in batches, blend until smooth. Taste and adjust seasonings as desired.

This sauce is quite thick, so add water by the tablespoon if you require a thinner consistency.

Makes 1 cup (250 mL)

1 tsp coconut oil
1/4 cup (60 mL) grated onion
1/2 cup (125 mL) finely grated carrot

1/4 tsp ground cumin
1/4 tsp garlic powder
1/8 tsp chile flakes

1 tbsp tomato sauce or ketchup
2 tbsp soy sauce
1/2 tsp Asian hot sauce
1/4 cup (60 mL) natural peanut butter

1 tsp lime juice
1/4 cup (60 mL) unsweetened nondairy milk

salt and freshly ground black pepper, to taste

Rutabaga Pizza / Pasta Sauce gf

Kid-approved, this mild but intensely tomato-flavored sauce is perfect tossed with pasta, as a dipping sauce, or spread on your favorite crust for a quick pizza. The recipe makes a lot, but freezes well, so save some for another day.

Makes 4 cups (1 L)

1/2 cup (125 mL) sun-dried tomatoes (not oil-packed)

1 tbsp olive oil
1 medium onion, finely chopped
2 packed cups (500 mL) peeled and grated rutabagas

1/4 cup (60 mL) red wine

1/3 cup (80 mL) tomato paste
1 tsp dried basil
1/2 tsp dried oregano
1/2 tsp garlic powder
1/2 tsp salt, or to taste
1/8 tsp freshly ground black pepper, or to taste

3 cups (750 mL) canned diced tomatoes
1 1/2 cups (375 mL) tomato juice

In a small bowl, cover sun-dried tomatoes with ½ cup (125 mL) boiling water and let sit for 10 minutes. Do not drain.

In a large pot on medium, heat oil. Sauté onions and rutabagas for 10 minutes, until soft, lightly browned, and reduced by half in volume. Deglaze pot with red wine.

Add soaked sun-dried tomatoes, their soaking water, tomato paste, basil, oregano, garlic powder, salt, and pepper. Sauté for 1 minute. Add diced tomatoes and tomato juice. Bring to a boil. Reduce heat to medium and simmer, stirring occasionally, for 20–25 minutes, until rutabaga is completely tender and flavors are well combined.

Using an immersion blender or in a countertop blender, working in batches, purée until smooth. Taste and adjust seasoning as desired.

If the finished sauce is too thick, thin with more tomato juice or add stock. If it's is too thin, simmer on medium until thickened.

Horseradish Crema gf

This sauce adds rich and creamy zing to anything. I especially like it served with Golden Chili (p. 174) and Sweet Potato & Pinto Bean Enchiladas (p. 145) for a burst of heat that refreshes.

From can of coconut milk, remove solid white portion and place in large bowl. Reserve clear liquid for another use.

In a large bowl, by hand or with a hand mixer on medium, beat solid coconut milk until light and fluffy, about 3 minutes. Add juice, salt, and pepper. Beat to fully incorporate.

Add grated horseradish by the tablespoon. Whisk to incorporate and taste after each addition. Taste and adjust seasoning as desired.

Makes about 1 cup (250 mL)

1 450-mL (15-oz) can full-fat coconut milk, refrigerated overnight

1 1/2 tbsp freshly squeezed lime juice
1/2 tsp salt
1/8 tsp freshly ground black pepper

2–4 tbsp grated fresh horseradish

With horseradish a little goes a long way.

- Always add to taste, starting with less than specified and adding more as desired. This potent root brings brightness to any dish and can clear your sinuses if too much is used.

- Always remove skin, which is tough and unpleasant. The whiter the flesh, the fresher the root.

- To avoid an overly bitter taste, use the horseradish within 20 minutes of being grated. This also ensures maximum potency.

- Try using fresh wasabi (which is related to horseradish and also known as Japanese horseradish), if it's available.

Sesame Horseradish Dipping Sauce gf

This is a wonderful way to add the intense flavor of horseradish (or wasabi if it's fresh) to your dippers. Try this fiery, salty thick dip on sushi or spring rolls or tossed through cooked Asian noodles.

In a small frying pan on medium, toast seeds for 3–4 minutes, until fragrant and white seeds are golden. Remove 1 tsp assorted seeds and set aside.

Place remaining seeds in a spice grinder or food processor and grind to a powder. Transfer to a small bowl. Add soy sauce, vinegar, sesame oil, and 1 tbsp water to bowl. Mix well. Add horseradish to bowl and mix well.

Sprinkle with reserved sesame seeds.

Makes ½ cup (125 mL)

2 tbsp white sesame seeds
1 tbsp black sesame seeds
1 tsp coriander seeds

2 tbsp soy sauce
2 tbsp rice wine vinegar
1 1/2 tbsp sesame oil

2–4 tbsp grated fresh horseradish

Islands Dressing gf

*I have mentioned in my previous books how much my husband loves Thousand Island dressing—
I'm always searching for new variations to meet his exacting standards. He loved this one!*

In a small bowl, mix all ingredients until well combined. Taste and adjust seasoning as desired. Chill for at least 1 hour before using.

The consistency of the dressing depends on the mayonnaise used; just thin with 1 tsp water if needed. This dressing will last in the refrigerator for up to 5 days, so make it on a quiet weekend for the busy week ahead.

Makes about 1 ½ cups (375 mL)

1 cup (250 mL) Sweet Potato Mayo (p. 192)
  or other vegan mayonnaise
5 tbsp minced Radish & Daikon Pickle
  (p. 199)
2 tbsp Rutabaga Pizza / Pasta Sauce (p. 186)
  or tomato sauce
1 tbsp liquid from Radish & Daikon Pickle
  or red wine vinegar
1 tbsp minced capers

salt and freshly ground black pepper, to
  taste

Sweet Potato Mayo gf

Oil-free and luscious, this dressing is tangy, creamy, and smooth, with a hint of sweetness.

Makes 2 cups (500 mL)

1 medium white-flesh sweet potato

8 oz (230 g) soft tofu, drained
4–5 tbsp fresh lemon juice
2 1/2 tbsp apple cider vinegar
2 tsp Dijon mustard
1 tsp lemon zest
1 1/4 tsp salt
1/8 tsp freshly ground black pepper

Preheat oven to 400°F (200°C).

Prick sweet potato with a fork and bake for 60–75 minutes, until completely tender. Remove from oven and allow to cool completely. This step may be completed in advance.

Halve sweet potato and scoop out 1 cup (250 mL) flesh. Place in food processor and add tofu, 4 tbsp lemon juice, cider vinegar, mustard, lemon zest, salt, and pepper. Blend until smooth, stopping to scrape down sides of bowl as required.

Taste and adjust seasoning as desired, adding 1 tbsp more lemon juice for extra tang.

To make horseradish mayo, simply add 1–2 tbsp freshly peeled and grated horseradish to ¼ cup (60 mL) Sweet Potato Mayo or your favorite mayonnaise. It adds a powerful pop to any sandwich or burger.

Kohlrabi & Mushroom Gravy gf

Savory and comforting, this is a great vehicle for sneaking in an introduction to kohlrabi. It also makes a wonderful meal with mashed potatoes.

In a medium saucepan on medium, heat oil. Sauté kohlrabi and mushrooms for 15 minutes, until mushrooms are dry, kohlrabi is soft, and both lightly browned. Vegetables will be reduced by three-quarters in volume.

Add garlic and thyme, and sauté for 30 seconds, until fragrant. Add margarine, soy sauce, yeast, and vinegar. Stir to combine and melt margarine. Stir in potato flour and cook for 1 minute to form a roux (a thick paste).

Add ½ cup (125 mL) stock, and stir well to combine and thicken. Add ½ cup (125 mL) stock, and repeat until all stock is added. Stir in creamer, and cook for 1 minute to fully combine and thicken.

Don't discard the mushroom gills — they add depth of color and flavor to the gravy.

The recipe can be made in advance. Gently reheat before serving.

Makes 2 cups (500 mL)

1 tbsp olive oil

8 oz (230 g) kohlrabi, peeled and grated, greens removed

1 Portobello mushroom, grated

2 garlic cloves, finely grated

1/2 tsp dried thyme

1 tbsp vegan margarine

1 1/2 tbsp soy sauce

1/2 tbsp nutritional yeast

1 1/4 tsp balsamic vinegar

2 tbsp potato flour

1 1/2 cups (375 mL) mushroom or vegetable stock

1/4 cup (60 mL) soy creamer

Beet Tapenade *gf*

Salty and briny, yes, but with background notes of earthy sweetness — hard to stop eating off the spoon right out of the food processor. Will go with any pasta dish, antipasto platter, even grilled tofu.

Makes 1 ¼ cups (310 mL)

2 small beets, scrubbed and trimmed

1/2 cup (125 mL) black olives, pitted
1/2 cup (125 mL) Kalamata olives, pitted
1 tbsp olive oil
1 tbsp olive brine (liquid from jar)
1 1/2 tbsp capers
1 garlic clove, roughly chopped
1/8 tsp freshly ground black pepper

salt and freshly ground black pepper, to
   taste

Preheat oven to 400°F (200°C).

Prick beets with a fork, wrap individually in aluminum foil and bake for 1–1 ¼ hours, depending on their size, until perfectly tender. Remove from oven, unwrap foil, and allow to cool, about 30 minutes.

Rub peel off beets, then roughly chop and place in food processor along with both kinds of olives, olive oil, brine, capers, garlic, and pepper. Pulse until finely chopped and well combined but not smooth.

Taste and season with salt and pepper as desired.

In order to avoid having the oven on for an hour just to cook 2 beets, plan ahead and roast them while you bake something else.

→ *Eat Your Greens*

Staying true to a vegetable means using as many parts as possible—a root to tip style of eating. Many of my recipes use edible greens that are readily available. Here is a guide that lists which greens can and cannot be safely eaten.

Eat these greens raw or cooked:

beets

carrots

celeriac

daikon

kohlrabi

radish

rutabagas

sweet potatoes

turnips

Never eat these greens, which are toxic:

burdock

jicama

parsnips

potatoes

sunchokes

yuca

many tropical yams (best to avoid them all)

water chestnuts

Avocado & Jicama Pico de Gallo

Crisp fresh jicama adds a new textural and flavor dimension to this staple dip. Wonderful alongside crudités or a cooked dish such as Sweet Potato & Pinto Bean Enchiladas (p. 145).

Makes about 2 cups (500 mL)

1/3–1/2 cup (80–125 mL) peeled and finely
  diced jicama
1 medium avocado, pitted, peeled and
  diced
2 tbsp lime juice

1/4 cup (60 mL) finely chopped red onions
2 medium tomatoes, seeded and finely
  chopped
1 jalapeño, seeded and finely chopped
2 tbsp finely chopped cilantro leaves
1/2 tsp agave syrup
1/4 tsp salt

In a medium bowl, toss jicama and avocado in lime juice. Let sit while you chop other vegetables.

Add red onions, tomatoes, jalapeño, cilantro, syrup, and salt to jicama and avocadoes. Stir gently to combine, trying to keep avocado pieces intact. Cover and refrigerate for 1 hour to allow flavors to develop before serving.

If you like food that's not very spicy, start with half a jalapeño, taste, then add more if desired.

Lemon Walnut Beet Green Pesto

A vibrant, fresh, clean-tasting pesto, perfect on roasted beets or pasta, and alongside Baked Beet Cakes (p. 67) or Carrot & White Bean Croquettes (p. 63), any time you want an uplifting taste of lemon paired with basil and beet greens.

In a blender or food processor, purée all ingredients in order given until smooth, stopping to scrape down sides of bowl as required.

If you prefer a thinner consistency, add water 1 tbsp at a time, blending after each addition until desired consistency is reached.

Taste and adjust seasoning as desired.

You'll need the leaves from a medium bunch of beets. If possible, choose smallest leaves first, as they are softer and less intensely beet-flavored.

Makes about 1 cup (250 mL)

1 cup (250 mL) packed beet green leaves, stems and spines removed

1/2 cup (125 mL) packed fresh basil

1/2 cup (125 mL) walnut pieces

1/4 cup (60 mL) freshly squeezed lemon juice

3 tbsp flaxseed oil

1 tbsp nutritional yeast

1 small garlic clove, roughly chopped

1 small shallot (tbsp-sized), roughly chopped

1 tbsp lemon zest

1 tsp agave syrup

salt and freshly ground black pepper, to taste

Radish & Daikon Pickle gf

This is so pretty and pink, it could be an '80s movie. An ingredient in Islands Dressing (p. 191), this pickle is also a perfect stand-alone condiment with burgers, sausages, and sandwiches.

In a medium saucepan, combine all vinegars, syrup, salt, cumin seeds, and bay leaf. Heat on medium for 3–4 minutes, until syrup is melted and ingredients are combined.

Gently stir in sliced vegetables. Liquid will just cover them. Bring to a boil and cook for 1 minute. Remove from heat and let sit at room temperature, until completely cool, about 45 minutes.

Transfer to a glass container and refrigerate. Remove bay leaf before using.

Make in advance. The longer that this pickle sits in the refrigerator, the better the flavor.

Makes 1 cup (250 mL)

1/2 cup (125 mL) unseasoned rice vinegar
1/4 cup (60 mL) apple cider vinegar
1/4 cup (60 mL) white vinegar
3 tbsp brown rice syrup
1/2 tsp salt
1/2 tsp cumin seeds
1 bay leaf

1/2 cup (125 mL) very thinly sliced radishes, 2 large or 3 medium
1/2 cup (125 mL) halved and very thinly sliced daikon, cut in half-moon shapes
1/2 medium red onion, halved and thinly sliced

Celeriac Bacon *gf*

Straight out of the oven, these are crisp yet chewy with a smoky, salty, savory flavor like "real" bacon. As they sit, they're a little less crispy, a little chewier, and just as delicious.

Preheat oven to 425°F (220°C). Line 2 baking sheets with parchment paper.

In a large bowl, whisk together olive oil, soy sauce, liquid smoke, sesame oil, Marmite, garlic powder, paprika, and fennel seeds.

Halve and peel celeriac. Using a mandoline or a very sharp knife, cut slices no more than ⅛-in (3-mm) thick. Add slices to bowl and coat evenly.

Spread slices in single layers on prepared sheets. Bake for 10 minutes, remove from oven, turn slices over, and return sheets to oven, rotating rack position. Bake for 5 minutes, until slices are reduced by two-thirds in volume, dry looking, crisp around the edges, and slightly caramelized.

Makes 4 servings

2 tbsp olive oil

1 tbsp soy sauce

1 1/2 tsp liquid smoke

1/4 tsp sesame oil

1/4 tsp Marmite or miso (optional)

1/4 tsp garlic powder

1/8 tsp smoked paprika

1/8 tsp ground fennel seeds

1 1/2 lb (750 g) celeriac

Truly Decadent Desserts

Yes, even desserts! These treats, infused with the natural sweetness of root vegetables, will blow you away with never-before-thought-of uses for these humble roots. In these dishes, root vegetables are "ugly" no longer.

Salted Almond & Potato Macaroons

Marzipan-esque, almost like amaretti, these moist Christmas-y treats are oil-free (Santa will thank you). These are more like a Scottish macaroon (made traditionally with potatoes) than the French macaron, often misnamed as macaroon.

Preheat oven to 400°F (200°C). Prick potato with fork, wrap in aluminum foil, and bake for 75–85 minutes, until perfectly tender. Remove from oven and reduce oven temperature to 350°F (180°C). Line two baking sheets with parchment paper.

Let potato cool enough to handle, then halve and remove flesh. You should have 1 cup (250 mL). Transfer to a large bowl. Add almond extract and mash until very smooth with no lumps. Add ground almonds, flour, and confectioner's sugar. Mix carefully until well combined and smooth. Stir in slivered almonds.

Drop mixture 1 tbsp at a time on baking sheet, placing 1 in (2.5 cm) apart (the cookies do not spread). Bake for 20–22 minutes, until bottoms are browned and tops are golden. Cool for 5 minutes on sheet, then transfer to a rack to cool completely.

Once completely cooled, melt chocolate in microwave or double boiler, stirring until smooth. Dip tops of macaroons in melted chocolate and return to rack. Sprinkle with a little salt, then top with toasted almond slivers.

Set chocolate at room temperature or in the refrigerator. Return to room temperature before serving.

Reserve the skins from the baked potato for Potato Skins (p. 108).

Makes about 40 macaroons

1 large white potato

1/4 tsp almond extract

1 1/2 cups (375 mL) ground almonds
1 1/2 cups (375 mL) all-purpose flour
3 cups (750 mL) sifted confectioner's sugar

1 cup (250 mL) slivered almonds

1 1/4 cups (310 mL) chocolate chips or 10 oz (300 g) chopped bar chocolate

3–4 pinches flaked sea salt
1/4 cup (60 mL) toasted slivered almonds

Red Velvet Swirl Coffee Cake

To enjoy with coffee, this moist, rich cake is subtly flavored with chocolate, swirled with berry jam, and topped with a crumb, as all good coffee cakes should be. The red velvet color comes from reduced beet juice.

Makes 8-in (20-cm) square cake

Note: Juicer needed

2 cups (500 mL) beet juice

Crumb Topping
1/2 cup (125 mL) all-purpose flour
3 tbsp granulated sugar
1 tsp cocoa powder

2 tbsp vegan margarine

Cake
1 1/2 cups (375 mL) + 3 tbsp all-purpose
  flour
2 tbsp potato starch
1 1/2 tbsp natural cocoa powder
2 tsp baking powder
1 tsp baking soda
1/2 tsp salt

1 tsp vanilla extract
1/2 cup (125 mL) chocolate nondairy milk

1 cup (250 mL) granulated sugar
1/2 cup (125 mL) margarine

2 tbsp mixed berry jam

Make beet juice reduction

In a large saucepan on high, bring juice to a boil, reduce heat to medium, and cook for 30 minutes until reduced by half in volume to 1 cup (250 mL). Remove from heat and allow to cool to room temperature, 30 minutes.

While juice reduces and cools, make crumb topping.

Make topping

In a medium bowl, stir together flour, sugar, and cocoa. Rub in margarine to form crumb-like texture. Set aside.

Make cake

Preheat oven to 375°F (190°C). Line an 8-in (2-L) baking pan with parchment paper, leaving an overhang for removing coffee cake after baking.

In a medium bowl, sift together flour, potato starch, cocoa powder, baking powder, baking soda, and salt. Set aside. Once beet juice reduction is cool, stir in vanilla and chocolate milk.

In a large bowl, cream sugar and margarine until light and fluffy, about 2–3 minutes. Add sifted dry ingredients alternating with liquid ingredients to creamed mixture, stirring to just combine and when batter no longer looks curdled after each addition.

Scrape batter into prepared baking pan and spread to distribute evenly. Dot surface with teaspoon measures of jam. Using a skewer or fork, randomly swirl jam onto surface of cake. Dust top with crumb topping and gently press to lightly incorporate into top layer of batter.

Bake for 35–40 minutes, until a toothpick inserted in center of cake comes out clean. Cool in pan for 5 minutes, then lift from pan using parchment overhang and transfer to a rack to cool completely.

Coconut Sweet Potato Pie

With a not-too-sweet-creamy filling and a crisp I-wish-this-was-a-cookie crust, this decadent pie with Lemon-Infused Vegan Whipcream (p. 212) makes an ordinary day seem like a holiday. Best if prepared a day before serving.

Make crust

Preheat oven to 400°F (200°C). Oil a 9-in (23-cm) pie plate.

In a large bowl, mix together panko, ground almonds and pecans, brown sugar, cinnamon, and salt. Make a well. Add coconut oil to well and rub in to combine well. With dampened hands, press into base and sides of prepared pie plate.

Bake for 10 minutes until edges are browned and crust is fragrant and a little puffy. Remove from oven and, using the back of a spoon, press puffy crust back into sides and base of pie plate. Let cool as you prepare filling.

Make filling

In a large saucepan, combine grated sweet potatoes, coconut milk, dates, syrup, cinnamon stick, cloves, sumac, salt, nutmeg, and allspice. Bring to a boil, reduce heat to medium-low, and simmer, stirring occasionally, until sweet potatoes are tender and dates plumped, about 12 minutes. Remove cinnamon stick and cloves.

In a small bowl, whisk together agar powder with 2 tbsp water until smooth. Into agar water, whisk 2 tbsp cooked mixture from saucepan. Once combined, transfer agar mixture into saucepan and cook, stirring frequently, for 5 minutes, until thickened.

Transfer to a food processor or blender and purée until smooth. Pour filling onto cooled pie crust. Cool at room temperature for 20 minutes, then transfer to refrigerator to fully set.

Makes 8–10 servings

Crust

1 cup (250 mL) panko or gluten-free breadcrumbs

1/2 cup (125 mL) ground almonds

1/2 cup (125 mL) ground pecans

1/2 cup (125 mL) brown sugar

1/2 tsp ground cinnamon

1/4 tsp salt

1/2 cup (125 mL) softened (not melted) coconut oil

Filling

3 cups (750 mL) peeled and finely grated white-fleshed sweet potatoes

2 cups (500 mL) full-fat coconut milk

1/2 cup (125 mL) pitted Medjool dates, about 5

1/4 cup (60 mL) agave syrup

1 3-in (8-cm) length cinnamon stick

2 whole cloves

1/4 tsp ground sumac

1/4 tsp salt

1/8 tsp ground nutmeg

1/8 tsp ground allspice

1 tsp agar powder

Turnip Rum Raisin Cake

Lightly spiced, this pretty golden cake is studded with sweet, rum-soaked raisins and topped with a tangy sour cream icing.

Makes 10–12 servings

1/4 cup (60 mL) raisins
1/4 cup (60 mL) golden raisins
1/2 cup (125 mL) golden rum

1 1/2 cups (375 mL) nondairy milk
2 tbsp apple cider vinegar

1/4 cup (60 mL) neutral-flavored oil
3/4 cup (175 mL) brown sugar
1 cup (250 mL) finely grated turnips

2 1/4 cups (530 mL) all-purpose flour
2 1/2 tsp baking powder
1/2 tsp baking soda
1/2 tsp salt
1/2 tsp ground ginger
1/8 tsp turmeric

Icing

2 tbsp vegan margarine
1/3 cup (80 mL) vegan sour cream
1/2 tsp vanilla extract

2 cups (500 mL) confectioner's sugar, sifted
  if lumpy
1/4 tsp ground ginger

In a small bowl, combine both types of raisins and rum. Let sit for 30 minutes for raisins to plump and soften. Do not drain.

Preheat oven to 350°F (180°C). Line an 8-in (20-cm) springform pan with parchment paper.

In a large bowl, combine milk and vinegar. Let sit for 5 minutes to curdle. Add oil, sugar, turnips, and raisin-rum mixture to curdled milk and mix to combine.

Sift in flour, baking powder, baking soda, salt, ginger, and turmeric. Mix to just combine. Spoon batter into prepared pan and bake for 55 minutes, until cake has pulled away from the sides, is golden brown, firm to the touch, and a toothpick inserted in center of cake comes out clean. Cool for 10 minutes in pan, then remove outer ring and transfer to a rack to cool completely.

Make icing

In a medium bowl, cream margarine, sour cream, and vanilla extract. Stir in confectioner's sugar and ginger until smooth. When cake has cooled completely, ice top and drizzle decoratively down sides of cake.

Celeriac Brownies gf

Not just gluten-free but flour-free to boot. These perfectly sized-for-one treats (if only you could stop at one) are moist, rich, and soft with an intensely chocolate kick. Serve straight up or warm with vegan vanilla ice cream or Lemon-Infused Vegan Whipcream (p. 212).

Preheat oven to 400°F (200°C).

Prick celeriac, including cut sides, with a fork. Wrap in foil and bake for 90 minutes, until completely tender. Remove from oven and set aside until cool enough to handle. Scoop flesh from celeriac and transfer 1 cup (250 mL) to a food processor. Store remaining celeriac in refrigerator for another use.

Reduce oven to 350°F (180°C). Lightly oil a 12-cup muffin tin.

In a small bowl, combine chia seeds with ¼ cup (60 mL) water. Let sit 7-8 minutes, until thick and gloopy. Transfer to food processor.

In a large bowl, sift cocoa powder, confectioner's sugar, potato starch, baking powder, and salt. Make a well.

In food processor, pulse celeriac and chia mixture to combine and break up celeriac. Add melted coconut oil and chocolate chips, and vanilla extract, and purée until very smooth, stopping to scrape down sides of bowl as required.

Pour blended liquid ingredients into well in dry ingredients. Mix to just combine. Spoon batter into prepared muffin tin. The cups will be about half full.

Bake for 13–15 minutes, until edges are dry and pulling away from sides. Centers should look moist. Cool in muffin tin before removing.

Bake celeriac in advance, when oven is on for something else.

Makes 12

12 oz (340 g) celeriac, cut in half

1 tbsp ground chia seeds

1/2 cup (125 mL) cocoa powder
1/2 cup (125 mL) confectioner's sugar
3 tbsp potato starch or arrowroot powder
1 tsp baking powder
1/2 tsp salt

3 tbsp coconut oil, melted
1/4 cup (60 mL) chocolate chips, melted
1 tsp vanilla extract

Sweetly Spiced Rutabaga Pierogies

Reminiscent of pumpkin pie, these holiday-inspired treats will be a hit at the end of any dinner.
Serve with Lemon-Infused Vegan Whipcream on the side.

Makes 14 pierogies

8 oz (230 g) rutabaga, cut in half

Lemon-Infused Vegan Whipcream
1 15-oz (450-g) can full-fat coconut milk,
  chilled for 6 hours, preferably overnight

1/4 cup (60 mL) confectioner's sugar
1/2 tsp lemon zest
1/2 tsp lemon juice
1/4 tsp vanilla extract
pinch salt

Dough
1 cup (250 mL) all-purpose flour
2 tbsp potato flour
2 tbsp granulated sugar
1/4 tsp salt
pinch ground cinnamon
pinch ground ginger

2 tbsp melted vegan margarine

Preheat oven to 400°F (200°C). Prick rutabaga all over, including cut sides, with a fork. Wrap in foil and bake 1 ½ hours until tender. Cool to room temperature.

Make Whipcream

From chilled can of coconut milk, remove solid white portion and place in large bowl. Add 2 tbsp liquid coconut milk to bowl. Store remaining liquid in refrigerator for another use.

Add sugar, lemon zest and juice, vanilla extract, and salt to bowl. Using a whisk or handheld mixer, whip mixture for 4–5 minutes, until thick, creamy, and smooth. Refrigerate until required, and lightly re-whip before serving.

Make dough

In a large bowl, whisk together flours, sugar, salt, cinnamon, and ginger. Make a well and add melted margarine and 6 tbsp water. Mix well with hands to form a dough.

Turn onto lightly floured board and knead for 4 minutes, until elastic. Wrap in plastic wrap and let rest at room temperature for at least 30 minutes.

Make filling

Scoop 1 cup (250 mL) rutabaga flesh into large bowl. Mash until smooth. Add sugar, margarine, cinnamon, nutmeg, and ginger and mix well. Stir in flour to thicken.

Make pierogies

On a clean floured board, roll dough to $\frac{1}{16}$ in (1.5 mm) thickness. Using a 3-in (8-cm) round cookie cutter, cut out 14 circles, gathering and rolling scraps as required.

Gently stretch each circle to a 4-in (10-cm) diameter. The dough should stretch easily without tearing. Place a scant tablespoon of filling in center of dough circle and fold dough over filling, stretching it slightly as required and eliminating air pockets. Pinch to seal.

Place prepared pierogi on floured plate, and dust lightly with flour to prevent them from sticking and drying out. Continue to fill dough circles until all are filled, and filling is used up. Let pierogies rest for 20 minutes. (Pierogies can be frozen at this point and cooked from frozen later.)

Bring a large pot of salted water to a boil. Add pierogies in 2–3 batches (depending on size of pot) and boil for 2–3 minutes, until pierogies rise naturally to surface. This will take longer if cooking from frozen. Remove from water with a slotted spoon and drain.

In a large frying pan on medium-high, heat 1 tsp oil and 1 tsp margarine. Fry cooked pierogies in batches, adding more oil and margarine as necessary, 1–2 minutes per side, until they have a crisp and golden crust. Turn only once.

Plan ahead by refrigerating the can of coconut milk the day before you want to make the Whipcream.

Freeze pierogies after forming and before boiling. They can be boiled from frozen.

The boiling and frying can be done simultaneously. While one batch is frying, start boiling another.

Bake rutabaga in advance in oven when it's on for something else and refrigerate for up to 3 days.

Filling

1/2 cup (125 mL) brown sugar

2 tbsp vegan margarine

1/2 tsp ground cinnamon

1/4 tsp ground nutmeg

1/4 tsp ground ginger

6 tbsp all-purpose flour

1 tbsp neutral-flavored oil

1 tbsp vegan margarine

Carrot & Parsnip Fruit Mince

I have updated a traditional recipe with dried blueberries, cranberries, pineapple, and root vegetables. Use in the Christmas Cheesecake (p. 217), or make the Mince Tarts.

In a medium saucepan on medium, heat orange juice, brandy, and orange zest for 3–4 minutes, until almost boiling. Do not allow to boil. Remove from heat and stir in remaining ingredients. They will be just covered by the liquid.

Cover and let soak at room temperature for 3 hours, or until completely cool. Stir once or twice. Store in refrigerator. Let chill for 12 hours before using.

Christmas Mince Tarts

Traditional bites of fruity goodness—maybe you could save some for Santa.

Preheat oven to 375°F (190°C).

Fill tart shells with prepared fruit mince, and bake for 15–20 minutes, until outer edges of crusts are golden.

Serve warm or cold, dusted with a little confectioners' sugar.

For any dried fruits you don't like or can't find, please substitute a dried fruit of your preference in the same amount.

The mince can be made in advance and refrigerated in a covered container for up to 2 weeks.

Kitchen shears are easier and more efficient than a knife to cut ginger, dates, pineapple, and apricots.

When adding mince to recipes, first drain off excess liquid.

Makes 3 cups (750 mL)

1 1/4 cups (310 mL) orange juice
1/2 cup (125 mL) brandy, whiskey, or apple juice
1 tbsp orange zest

1 1/2 cups (125 mL) peeled and grated carrots
1 1/2 cups (125 mL) peeled and grated parsnips
1/4 cup (60 mL) currants
1/4 cup (60 mL) raisins
1/4 cup (60 mL) golden raisins
1/4 cup (60 mL) chopped dates
2 tbsp chopped crystallized ginger
2 tbsp mixed peel
2 tbsp chopped dried apricots
2 tbsp slivered almonds
2 tbsp chopped dried pineapple
2 tbsp dried cranberries
2 tbsp dried blueberries

Christmas Mince Tarts (makes 12)
12 unbaked mini tart shells
1 cup (250 mL) Carrot & Parsnip Fruit Mince

Christmas Cheesecake *gf* option *cn*

Christmas in New Zealand is in the summertime. While a heavy traditional Christmas cake is what many receive, it isn't always what they want. I invented this more weather-friendly version, though it's just as good in cold climes.

Make base

Lightly spray a 9-in (23-cm) springform pan with non-stick cooking spray. Clear space in your freezer for cake pan.

In a large bowl, mix together crumbs, ground almonds, potato starch, pie spice, cinnamon, nutmeg, and ginger. Make a well and add oil, syrup, and extracts. With clean hands, mix to combine well, then press firmly into prepared pan. Chill in freezer while preparing filling.

Make filling

Preheat oven to 350°F (180°C).

Drain excess liquid from fruit mince and place mince in a large bowl. Set aside.

In a blender, blend cream cheese and both types of tofu until very smooth and creamy, stopping to scrape down sides of jar as required. Add maple syrup, potato starch, lemon juice, molasses, and extracts to blender and process until very well mixed. Pour blended mix into fruit mince and stir to combine. Pour on top of chilled base.

Bake for 55–60 minutes, until edges are firm, lightly browned, and pulling away from sides of pan. Center should still jiggle a little.

Cool at room temperature for 30 minutes, then transfer to freezer for 1 hour. With a palette knife, cut around inside edge of springform pan to loosen cake before removing ring. Refrigerate (preferably overnight) to set completely before serving.

Plan ahead! This needs to be made the day before serving to allow setting time, and Carrot & Parsnip Fruit Mince (p. 215) needs to be made 24 hours before that.

Makes 12 servings

Base

1 3/4 cups (175 mL) vegan arrowroot biscuit or graham cracker crumbs (can be gluten-free)

1 cup (250 mL) ground almonds

1 tbsp potato starch or arrowroot powder

1/2 tsp pumpkin pie spice

1/4 tsp ground cinnamon

1/4 tsp ground nutmeg

1/4 tsp ground ginger

1/2 cup (125 mL) neutral-flavored oil

1/4 cup (60 mL) brown rice syrup

1/2 tsp vanilla extract

1/4 tsp almond extract

Filling

2 cups (500 mL) Carrot & Parsnip Fruit Mince (p. 215), made 24 hours in advance

12 oz (340 g) vegan cream cheese

8 oz (230 g) soft tofu

8 oz (230 g) firm tofu

6 tbsp maple syrup

1/4 cup (60 mL) potato starch

1 tbsp lemon juice

1 tbsp light molasses

1/2 tsp vanilla extract

1/4 tsp almond extract

Jicama & Asian Pear Tart

Not too sweet and wonderfully fresh, this dessert is reminiscent of a tarte tatin. The jicama and pears stay crisp, and there's a hint of sour lemon. This looks prettiest when prepared in a tart pan with fluted sides and a removable bottom, but made with a store-bought pie crust, it'll still taste fantastic.

Makes 8–10 servings

6 oz (175 g) soft tofu

1/2 cup (125 mL) plain or vanilla nondairy
  yogurt

1/2 cup (125 mL) granulated sugar

3 tbsp all-purpose flour

2 tbsp potato starch or cornstarch

1 tbsp lemon zest

1 tsp lemon extract

1 large Nashi (Asian) pear, peeled, cored,
  quartered, and cut into 1/8-in (3-mm)
  slices

1 small jicama, peeled, quartered, and cut
  into 1/8-in (3-mm) slices

1/2 cup (125 mL) lemon juice

1 uncooked pie crust in an 11-in (28-cm) tart
  pan with a removable bottom or a 9-in
  (23-cm) pie plate

1/4 cup (60 mL) brown sugar

3 tbsp vegan margarine, melted

6 tbsp all-purpose flour

Preheat oven to 400°F (200°C).

In a food processor or blender, blend tofu, yogurt, sugar, flour, potato starch, lemon zest, and lemon extract until thick and smooth, stopping to scrape down sides of bowl or jar as required. Pour into a large bowl and set aside.

In another large bowl, combine pear and jicama slices with lemon juice and toss to coat. Drain excess lemon juice, then place slices in bowl with tofu mixture. Toss to coat.

On bottom of pie crust, arrange coated pear and jicama slices in a pretty spiral pattern, if desired, or place randomly. Pour remaining tofu mixture over pear and jicama slices. Tart will be full.

Bake for 15 minutes, then reduce oven temperature to 350°F (180°C) and bake for 15 more minutes.

When tart is almost baked, mix brown sugar, melted margarine, and flour in a small bowl.

Remove tart from oven and spread topping on tart. Return to oven and bake for 30–35 minutes, until topping is puffy and golden, and filling is firm and bubbling. Cool in tart pan for at least 15 minutes before serving, or serve cold.

Asian pears are also known as Nashi, Korean, brown, and apple pears.

Jicama & Melon Fruit Salad gf raw

A sweetly singing salad when melons are at their peak. Tell everyone it's a three-melon salad with a new type of white melon.

In a medium bowl, toss jicama in vinegar and agave syrup. Let sit for 10 minutes while you prepare fruit.

Add melons, mint, salt and pepper chile flakes and stir to combine. Cover and refrigerate for 1 hour to develop flavor before serving

If you have any leftover salad, blend with water or juice until smooth, and serve over ice for a refreshingly different summer pick-me-up.

Makes 4 ½ cups (125 mL)

1 3/4 cups (175 mL) peeled and finely
  chopped jicama
1 tbsp white balsamic or apple cider vinegar
1 tbsp agave syrup

1 1/2 cups (375 mL) cubed cantaloupe
1 1/2 cups (375 mL) cubed honeydew melon
1 tbsp shredded fresh mint
1/4 tsp salt
pinch chile flakes, to taste

Acknowledgments

I always find this section the easiest to write—maybe because I have so many wonderful people to thank and to whom I am grateful.

In order to get the recipes to a point where they work, I have a dedicated team of testers. Some of these fine folks have tested for all four of my books, and I really couldn't do it without them. Located all over the world, they make the dishes and provide feedback. In doing so, they make the recipes that much better.

Liz Wyman, England

Anna B. Holt and her sons, England

Shirley Saliniemi, Finland

Linda Findon, Rotorua, New Zealand

Penny T, Melbourne, Australia

Amy Silver, Auckland, New Zealand

Fiona Wellgreen, Wellington, New Zealand

Kelly Cavalier, Ontario, Canada

Leah Holland, British Columbia, Canada

Trish Mounsey, British Columbia, Canada

Brenda McCorquodale, British Columbia, Canada

Courtney Blair, Massachusetts, United States

Debyi Kucera, Arizona, United States

Stefanie Amman, Oregon, United States

Jim Dwyer, Maine, United States

Carrie Lynn Morse, New Jersey, United States

My local crew of recipe tasters, who eat my leftovers and let me know what they like (obviously, everything!)

Starla Beselt

Nancy Macdonald

Paulette Taje

Jennifer Chutter

Karen Jackson

Thanks to Brian and Arsenal Pulp Press for agreeing to run with my idea of a book based on the weird and wonderful world of root vegetables—keeping it true.

To the APP production team: Susan, for making my words sound better, and Gerilee, for making them look better—I am eternally thankful. To Cynara, who gets the word out and arranges for the books to be seen everywhere—keep doing what you do.

For making my food look like it's truly worth a million bucks, many thanks to Tracey from Foodie Photography. No tricks employed in these photos—it's all real.

Finally, and always, to my family: You make everything worthwhile.

Index

Carla Kelly is an experienced vegan cook and baker who believes food tastes best when it is shared with laughter and love. A vegan for more than ten years, she has cooked at hotels around the world. She is the author of *Quick and Easy Bake Sale*, *Quick and Easy Vegan Slow Cooking*, and *Vegan al Fresco*. She blogs at the food website The Year of the Vegan, tweets @veganyearCarla, and can be found on Instagram @veganyear, and Facebook at Carla.Kelly.Vegan.